'In eight beautifully crafted stories, the aut
of culture, authority, succession, transitio...,
alignment are based on underlying and often unconscious emotions of
fear, anxiety, envy, uncertainty, abandonment. The resulting defences
(denial, blame, splitting, pairing, collusion etc.) blur the view of the
"real" problem, which needs to be solved by the client. "Not-Knowing"
is at the core of psychodynamically informed organisational consulting.
The authors demonstrate well how this difficult to achieve but necessary
attitude provides them with better interventions and thus solutions for
their clients. This book is a highly valuable, reflective, inviting, and
entertaining resource for leaders searching for consultancy and for
experienced and more recently trained consultants and coaches.'
**Professor Dr Claudia Nagel, Vrije Universiteit, Amsterdam,
Managing Partner Nagel & Company, Germany, consulting and
coaching for the top executive level**

'For those leaders who believe that people are the ultimate source
of sustainable competitive differentiation, this book is a must-read.
The humility and vulnerability displayed by the authors in their
storytelling is unusual. It invites the readers to slow down, reflect on
their own biases, to look at "what lies beneath" the surface of their
organisation, and to avoid jumping too quickly to solutions. These
"checks and balances" are the conditions for both identifying and
dealing with the root causes of problems. In our changing context,
this book is a timely reminder that strong relationships are the
cornerstone of good business.'
Xavier Isaac, CEO, Accuro Fiduciary Group

WHAT LIES BENEATH

WHAT LIES BENEATH
How Organisations *Really* Work

Ajit Menon and Trevor Hough

PHOENIX
PUBLISHING HOUSE
firing the mind

Cover by Jamie Lyon. Jamie is a student artist from Oxfordshire, England. His compositions are highly imaginative and aesthetic, with a particular emphasis on the exploration of human emotions. His work has been displayed at the National Portrait Gallery in London.

First published in 2021
by Phoenix Publishing House Ltd
62 Bucknell Road
Bicester
Oxfordshire OX26 2DS

British Library Cataloguing in Publication Data

A C.I.P. for this book is available from the British Library

ISBN-13: 978-1-912691-92-0

Typeset by vPrompt eServices Pvt Ltd, India

Printed in the United Kingdom

www.firingthemind.com

Contents

Confidentiality

The stories in this book, whilst based on our consulting practice, are ficticious and the identifying details have been been anonymised to preserve confidentiality and anonymity of characters they have been based on. The case stories are a composite of individuals and organisations presenting similar dynamics. Any resemblance to individuals or organisations is purely coincidental.

Acknowledgements

Writing a book is so often described as a solitary affair; however, this book has been far from that. It has come about as the result of many previous relationships. Usually, people co-author books after years of friendship, but the two of us took the opposite course—we became good friends after writing the book together.

There have been so many amazing people who have assisted and contributed to this book in so many ways and our apologies for not naming you individually. However, the following people we would like to thank personally.

Ajit

Jack Pijl, you have stood by me and read and re-read multiple versions of our manuscript with patience and a supportive yet critical eye.

Andy Lyon, friend and sparring partner, you have been instrumental in pushing us to think beyond our theoretical dogma and consider the realities of the consulting enviroment.

Dr. Caryn Solomon, you have mentored, developed and taught me all I have needed to know to be an expert OD practitioner.

Trevor

My parents Terry and Gail Hough, thank you for providing the most wonderful experience of being a nomad early in my life. Allowing me the space and opportunity to explore and experience this wide planet.

Professor Dreyer Kruger, wherever you are out there in the ether right now, thank you for your counsel, mentorship and friendship. For being a male role model in a world where I found so few. I will never ever forget your ever present counsel—*"Trevor, tell them to all f*** off!"*

Micky Stern, the woman who helped a lost young boy to grow up and find his sense of self. Who showed me what relatedness is really about. I am truly humbled and grateful for what we have shared for over 18 years.

About the authors

Ajit Menon is a business psychologist and consultant with many years of experience consulting to organisations of all sizes and complexities. He started his career in India, and then subsequently moved to the UK, where he worked as an organisation development consultant in the financial services. Over his career he has consulted to a range of organisations from banks, media, insurance, private equity to criminal justice and government. Ajit is the co-founder of Blacklight Advisory Ltd, a specialist organisational consultancy to a diverse range of clients. He specialises in organisational culture and works with leaders to create an environment to support businesses to thrive and adapt to their changing contexts. This interest came from his early research into culture in diasporic communities in Kenya. Ajit has been visiting faculty on organisation development and consultancy at the London School of Economics and the Tavistock and Portman NHS Trust. His passion is working with leaders to solve complex organisational problems related to culture and behavioural change.

Trevor Hough is a clinical psychologist, executive coach, and organisation development consultant. Trevor grew up as a nomad living all over the world and through this developed a keen interest in diverse cultural experiences. After his clinical training as a psychologist, Trevor worked as a psychotherapist in Cape Town for a few years before the nomadic voice within him spoke up. Trevor has been consulting to a diverse range of organisations globally for the last 15 years. These have included organisations from financial services, alternative energy and recycling companies as well as big retail concerns. Trevor has a strong interest in working with impact investment portfolio companies and has worked extensively with such organisations in Africa, India and Asia. Trevor works with Ajit as a principal consultant at Blacklight Advisory Ltd. Outside of his consulting work, Trevor's great passion is being out in nature. He has trained as a field and trails guide in the African bush and is in his element when out tracking animals on foot.

Foreword

Vega Zagier Roberts

This book invites you on a journey. Or rather, on eight journeys, from Mumbai to Paris and from fashion to finance. From the opening lines of each chapter, you accompany the authors from the landing of their flight or their trip on the Eurostar to meet their clients.

Often these journeys seem to have a clear roadmap at the outset. The client 'knows' what the problem is, and what is needed. So, they fly in these very experienced consultants, often thousands of miles, to bring their expertise and tools to provide this. When the consultants start following their hunch that something else might be going on and start exploring in more depth, there is often strong push-back from the client to stick to the initial brief and supply the intervention the client has already decided they need.

At the same time, in many of the stories, these particular consultants have been brought in because they and their way of working are already known to the organisation. Which suggests that at some level the client knows there is more going on than meets the eye—that which has been called 'the unthought known'. The client both wants and does not want to look at what 'lies beneath'. They want the consultants to agree to their own 'diagnosis' of what is needed, and they also want the consultants to make it feel safe enough to look deeper.

The terrain is complex, the invitations ambivalent. What Ronald Heifetz and his colleagues at Harvard have said about leadership is also true for consultants: that their key task is to enable people to face the hard choices confronting them—to challenge without getting pulled into providing 'easy answers'—but also to help them by making it more bearable to face what they have been avoiding. And as they put it, this will generate 'chaos, confusion and conflict', when what people think they need is certainty and quick solutions.

Many situations can be worked with by paying attention to what is visible and measurable, and can be addressed using known methods. These are often referred to as 'tame problems'. But 'wicked problems' cannot be clearly formulated: they involve multiple interdependent factors, many of which may well not be visible at the outset. This means working with data that is less immediately available, and may be overlooked when one feels driven to solve the problem before fully understanding it. And this demands something of leaders and consultants beyond expertise and familiar solutions.

First, it requires tolerating uncertainty. The pressure on leaders—and also on consultants—to 'know' is huge. When consultants are able to withstand this pressure, they also model something for their clients about the value of 'not knowing' until the situation has been explored in more depth. The poet Keats spoke of 'negative capability', the capability to bear 'being in uncertainties, mysteries, doubts, with any irritable [premature] reaching after fact and reason'. From this place, something new—something previously unknown—can emerge.

Second, it requires being in touch with 'what lies beneath'. The authors use the familiar metaphor of the iceberg, of which only about a tenth is visible above the water. But, as they point out, what lies below is not just a static mass of ice but a whole ecosystem. There are reefs and currents. Exploring under the surface carries risk, not least the risk of being caught up in the swirls and eddies. Often we defend ourselves by keeping our distance from the currents—the organisational dynamics—so as not to get swept away. When we can allow ourselves to be *in* the currents, to feel the undertow, we begin to get a first-hand sense of what is really going on.

Both uncertainty and getting caught in the currents make us vulnerable. And vulnerability often brings feelings of shame. Brené Brown,

American professor and author, speaks about 'the power of vulnerability' in what became one of the most watched TED talks of all time, with over 50 million views. This led to numerous invitations to speak to organisations, often with a request, please, not to talk about vulnerability or shame but rather about innovation and creativity. But, as she points out, it is precisely at those times when we dare to be vulnerable and to listen to our experiences of shame that we can become most creative.

The authors describe just such moments, when they find themselves buffeted by feelings of anger or confusion or an urge to blame. As experienced process consultants, they know that difficult feelings are often vital clues to what is going on, but that does not always make the feelings easy to bear. They are frank in acknowledging their feelings of embarrassment and shame when they get derailed and lose their way for a while. They also show how they use both consulting to themselves (in the section 'Consultant's reflections' in each chapter) and peer supervision to regain perspective.

A unique element of this book is the reporting of the actual peer-to-peer conversations between the authors, where the consultant not directly involved in the case helps the other delve deeper into the dynamics they have got caught up in. The authors call these conversations 'peer supervision'. Supervision is usually a very private space where outsiders cannot see in, but in this book the reader gets an insider perspective on the process of losing and re-finding one's way.

Rather than supervision, which comes from the Latin *super* (above) and *videre* (see), I prefer the term 'extravision', which captures the key element: having someone outside the immediate situation to help one think. This can, of course, be a manager or coach, but it can be a peer or even someone who is junior to oneself. We each have our own way of making sense of situations. We also each have our blind spots, particularly when we are caught up by the undertow, or when our defences are triggered. Having someone alongside who will challenge without judging, and whose blind spots are different from our own, can be invaluable in getting out of the undertow and bringing new perspectives into view. Heifetz, using the metaphor of the ballroom, calls this 'getting on the balcony': you need to spend time on the dance floor to really feel the music, but you then need to get on the balcony to see and make sense of the patterns that you cannot see when you are part of the dance.

In their conclusion, Ajit and Trevor speak about humility and curiosity as guiding principles. And they model these two principles throughout the book. As we try to make sense of situations that challenge us, can we stay curious (rather than beating ourselves up or blaming others), always asking the question, 'What else … and what else …?' And when our earlier sense-making is contradicted by new data, can we have the humility to let go of what may have felt to us—or impressed others—as great insights?

There are different ways to come along on these intriguing journeys. You can come as a passenger, reading the book as a kind of travelogue, finding resonances with experiences you have had yourself. Or you can choose to alight from time to time to consider your own moments of perplexity and derailment in more depth, using your emotional experiences to 'consult to yourself'. And when you have gone as far as you can on your own, you might want to think who could accompany you in diving deeper to help you uncover what lies beneath.

Vega Zagier Roberts, MD
Leadership coach, consultant and consultancy supervisor
Co-editor of *The Unconscious at Work*

Preparing for our journey

We thought it was important to start this book by introducing ourselves and our partnership. You will find that this book reads as a narrative, a collection of stories that are interwoven with our reflections and conversations. It is a tapestry made up of some of the experiences of our professional consulting lives. Our intention in choosing these specific stories and the thread that weaves them together is that these experiences show the complexity of working with organisational problems. In our opinion, they show how we as consultants can get caught up in and derailed by the dynamics of the organisational system. It is for this reason that we include our actual supervision conversations at the end of each chapter, for it is only through this that we believe we get to see how we get caught up in the system's dynamics.

We will start by introducing ourselves and our experience of each other.

Trevor's story

It was one of those crisp spring London mornings that greeted me as I walked out of the Covent Garden tube station. I had thirty minutes in which to slowly meander to our breakfast meeting. Most of the shops were still closed but the smell of freshly ground coffee wafted through the air as small patisseries slowly opened their doors.

It had been almost a year since Ajit and I had been introduced for the third time. It seemed that our colleagues were more convinced that we should meet than we were. Perhaps we were both wary of introductions in the consulting world, as most are not very subtle solicitations for work. However, our colleagues were persistent: 'You are both psychologists, you both work in financial services and work with what lies beneath the surface of organisations' was a line we heard often. We had numerous conversations and had tried to find a time when we were both in London, but this had not been easy. I had flown in from Cape Town over the weekend and Ajit had just arrived back from Dubai; we both had a day or two off, so we had no more excuses. Tuesday morning, 9.30 am at Ajit's workspace, was finally in both of our diaries.

He was sitting at the table drinking tea, smartly dressed in a 'Modi' jacket and jeans. He greeted me warmly with a handshake and enquired what I would like to drink. Having just returned from a trip to Mumbai, where I had been introduced to the 'Modi' jacket, I made small talk about his. 'You do know it's not really a "Modi" jacket, but rather a reinvention of the type of jacket first worn by Jawaharlal Nehru,' he said confidently. That response to my small talk has stayed with me and defined our relationship ever since: his ability to shift from surface chitchat to deeper, textured conversation with ease.

So began a two-hour conversation that moved from our consulting experiences to Freud's house in north London to the food theatre at a restaurant in Mumbai. It struck me that in those two hours neither of us tried to solicit work from the other. It reminded me of the Chinese tradition of *guān xì*—the principle that strong relationships are the cornerstone of good business. This was what both Ajit and I believed to be the bedrock of good leadership and strong organisations: strong, authentic and textured relationships.

Ajit's story

It had been a busy week and I had managed to get into London early that morning and found myself enjoying a purposeful but mindful walk from Charing Cross Station to Covent Garden. I was curious to meet Trevor. I had been introduced and reintroduced to him now about three times by different people. Our initial telephone conversation had been thought-provoking. I also knew that he worked in a sub-entity of a client system that I was working in as well. As I meandered through the cobblestoned roads of Covent Garden, I began thinking about a meeting I had held with a client the previous week. It had been a difficult interchange and I hadn't been able to make sense of what happened. I wondered if it might be interesting to throw around some ideas with Trevor.

He arrived at the meeting a few minutes before expected. He was shorter than I imagined but warm, gregarious—and loud! It was a meeting of minds as we started to explore areas of interests and work. We began to consider the client system that we both worked in and what emerged was a generative and challenging discussion. Very quickly, we established the trust required to have a truly vulnerable conversation about a client situation, which meant we could both learn and grow from it.

Our individual and joint consultancy journeys have taken many convoluted paths. We have consulted to organisations of all sizes, from all sectors and at many stages of development. From charities to large conglomerates, we have seen and experienced all sorts of organisational successes and challenges. We have experienced working with large retail organisations, diamond merchants, financial institutions, and charities. Despite our combined years of experience, every time we go into a client engagement, we find that we have something new to learn and we believe that it is this open, curious mindset that has helped us with our practice.

The context for this book

This book is a compilation of organisational stories based on our consulting experiences. We believe it is an honest account of cases we have encountered in our consulting practice. Each story is presented by one of us from the point of view of the consultant on the job. At the end of the story, we capture a dialogue between the authors in the form of a supervision conversation. This is intended to reflect on the consulting process and also on the dynamic between consultant and client. It also creates an additional space in which we invite you, the reader, to think about what is happening both in the organisation, between the consultant and the organisation, and also between the two authors.

We work in a field called organisation development (OD). This field has existed for many decades, with its genesis being in post-World War Two thinking on human relations. OD focuses on helping organisations, leaders and individuals to develop by engaging in a process of enquiry and intervention to transform their patterns of thought and behaviour. It encompasses a wide range of efforts designed to strengthen an organisation's capability to survive and thrive by changing that business's way of problem-solving. All this is done through a strong behavioural science framework.

Throughout this book, we will utilise the metaphor of an iceberg when describing what happens in organisations. As with an iceberg, what is seen—what is above the waterline—only relates to a small part of what is actually occurring. Organisational life is spent mainly attending to what is above the waterline. Strategy, systems, structure, and metrics have become the primary focus. Whilst these are a critical part of organisational make-up, what is not usually focused on is whatever is happening below the surface—the relational and cultural dynamics aspects of the organisation. This occurs for many reasons: it is difficult, it is revealing, and for the most part it is intangible and immeasurable. However, we believe strongly in the value of considering these elements whilst intervening and working within organisations.

Today, OD is concerned with building capacity and capability to manage change in an organisation. This is done through supporting organisational learning, leadership development, and helping organisations evolve and build their 'culture'. Many of the top business schools have developed faculties that on the whole tend to take on a more 'above the water' or behavioural methodology. They develop leaders and managers in specific skills in order for them to succeed in these roles and thereby enable successful organisations.

We are more interested in what happens within and around organisations; we focus on individual and group dynamics. An important part of the idea of dynamics is that it is often hidden and unconscious in the organisational system.

Another important focus of our work is organisational culture. The late Sumantra Ghoshal famously described culture as 'the smell of the place'. It is that intangible sense, the feeling that you get when you enter an organisation or a team setting. In the 1980s, Warner Burke contributed to the field by defining organisational development as a planned process of change in an organisation's culture. Culture started becoming a focal point in organisations and many OD consultants began to work on aligning culture, strategy, and organisation design.

There is no room to write a comprehensive thesis of culture here, but what we want to draw attention to is that culture is not a 'thing'. Cultures evolve and are difficult but not impossible to change. Culture is a socially constructed meaning system that is a part of any group. Group members are as much a part of the culture as they are immersed in it. Many authors suggest that leaders create the culture of their organisations. Edgar Schein says leaders play a role in building and managing the culture. Leaders become leaders in specific organisations precisely because they are part of and represent the dominant organisational culture. They model behaviours that are appropriate (or sometimes inappropriate) to the culture. Along with this, culture in groups and organisations is influenced heavily by the environment and context. Many have tried to simplify the concept of culture and promoted the idea that organisations can create unique internal cultures that are completely separate from what occurs around them. The idea of culture being an orchid inside a bell jar is a metaphor that relates to this idea. However, culture is not an object that can be seen; nor are the boundaries between people, organisations, and wider society as impermeable as glass. Each part of the cultural system impacts the next in a reciprocal manner.

Cultural dimensions are fundamental to our work, especially as many of the cultural norms and beliefs are usually unconscious but they are what 'run' the organisation. And, as consultants, it is incumbent upon us to pay close attention to the culture if we want to have an impact on organisational change. So, in our work we pay close attention to these factors and how they impact the organisation and its performance. You could say that the work we take up as OD consultants is akin to that of social anthropologists, and that we too utilise a participant observer role in organisations.

In no way do we believe that we have all the answers. The thing about dealing with the intangible is that there can be multiple realities based on which position one takes—and this is what makes it so difficult to work with. However, what we have found very useful in our work is the idea of supervision. Both of us have been in clinical or consulting supervision for most of our careers.

The concept of supervision and extravision

The idea of supervision comes from clinical and, more specifically, psychotherapy work. Early models of supervision can be traced to models of learning whilst doing. Educational frameworks where mistakes or blind spots are highlighted in the service of learning are aligned with this model. Usually a supervisor is a senior, more accomplished professional in the field who guides the supervisee in their practice. The supervisor is different to a mentor in that they provide specific feedback on a case-by-case basis rather than merely motivating and encouraging their apprentice.

Supervision in the field of psychotherapy has been shrouded in mystery and secrecy for much of its existence. Not much of what actually happens in supervision is written about. Part of this is obviously about patient or client confidentiality. However, much more originates in our minds, concerning the double-edged sword of going to supervision. On the one hand, it is a relief to receive assistance in managing a case; on the other hand, it can leave one in a vulnerable position by revealing how one actually works with a client. Feedback can be experienced as simultaneously useful and shaming, as what you are receiving feedback on is not merely your technique but who you are as a person.

We have taken peer supervision, or what the Grubb Institute calls 'extravision', as our model in this book, whereby we make our consulting stories available to scrutiny from each other. With extravision, what is important is not that the person you are working with is more experienced, but rather that it is someone who is outside of the actual work and not clouded by being part of the system being worked with. This person can be a peer or even someone less experienced than you. This can be of great value not only to consultants like ourselves, but to leaders in organisations.

For both of us, this has been a fantastic learning process as it evokes different emotions, reactions, and feelings than being supervised by someone who is more senior in the field. Extravision is a useful model as it means you have to be open to questions about your practice from a peer. This activates multiple defences, which are also worth paying attention to, as these can tell us a lot about what is going on in the dynamic of the consulting relationship.

The structure of this book

In a number of stories, the idea of succession or transition seems to emerge. These are about some of the most challenging and anxiety-provoking events in organisational life and we thought it important to focus on them. In other stories, you will witness the consultant's struggles with the task and the content of the work. The names and identifying details have been changed in all stories for the purposes of maintaining client confidentiality.

Chapter 1 is the story of an Indian property company through which we present our view of consulting and the primary framework that we use. Our work is based on strong academic and theoretical foundations, but we present the iceberg model as a simple metaphor through which to understand our thinking.

Chapter 2 is the story of an apparent cry for help from a British private banking client. It describes how the consultant may have got seduced into an unhelpful dynamic while trying to be helpful. From here on in the book, we introduce the idea of peer supervision.

Chapter 3, set in Hong Kong, is the story of an Australian software company where the consultant is pulled into a role within the organisation. It demonstrates the difficulty of maintaining role boundaries and what this can do to the consulting task.

Chapter 4 describes helping a client through a major role transition. Set in a South African national homeware retail organisation, this story is about the struggle that senior leaders can go through when dealing with the anxiety of role changes.

Chapter 5, set in Rio de Janeiro, is about the consultant's struggle to maintain authority whilst working in a consulting team. It describes the ways in which a consulting team can mirror a client system and how important this data is for the consultant to consider.

Chapter 6 is located in the Maasai Mara in Kenya. It is the story of an entrepreneurial team trying to grow their business. The importance of purpose, primary task, and also competing tasks are explored in this consultation.

Chapter 7 is set in a large fashion chain in Paris. The story describes how a consulting team can get split by a client system and what this means for the consulting intervention.

Chapter 8 describes the story of an Italian technological organisation in Milan and a founder CEO who is struggling to let go—and the impact of this on him, his immediate team, and the organisation.

This book is written for those who work in and with organisations—for founders and executives, for leaders and managers, and especially for those who work with or are considering working with external consultants such as ourselves. It is also written for those in leadership positions who take up roles we would call 'leader as consultant'. For all of those mentioned above, we hope that the methodology of storytelling and peer supervision provides some insight into the complexity of organisational life.

What Lies Beneath is not written as a theoretical text, but we hope that it does pique your curiosity and lead you to the myriad of wonderful books that are available on this subject. Our hope is that through these stories we can encourage interest and curiosity in a way of working with what lies beneath the surface in your organisations. We hope you enjoy this journey to the bottom of the iceberg and back as much as we have.

1. Mumbai

The clouds were building over the horizon and the Arabian Sea looked agitated in anticipation of the first rain. The air was already filled with the sweet smell of earth, signalling the arrival of the monsoon. From his office on the twenty-seventh floor, Rajat stood looking out at Mumbai. His room was plush, a testament to his success in building his business over the years. The large windows on one side allowed him to take in views of the sea. On the other was a vista of Mumbai's skyscrapers and glass buildings, flanked by the slums of Dharavi, reminding him of his own humble beginnings.

Rajat was the CEO (chief executive officer) of a real estate business that constructed commercial and residential buildings across India. He had started his business in the 1980s by taking out a small loan and putting up his own house as collateral; a risky decision at the time, but he had been convinced it would pay off. Despite his huge success, he still owned the original property he'd put up as collateral as a reminder of his roots.

He had designed his business to have a family feel and he was clearly the head of that family. He was revered as the patriarch of the business and even though the organisation was now 1,500 people strong, every new recruit—wherever they were hired—was known to him. He signed off all major property deals and was integral to every big decision.

Having grown and led his business over the years, he was now in a position to hand over the reins to the next generation.

Rajat had educated his son and daughter in some of the most prestigious universities in the world and they were now, in his opinion, ready to take on the business. In the past, both of his children had worked in other organisations at his insistence, so they could bring in valuable experience and skills from outside. Six months earlier, he had begun introducing them into some of the senior decision-making forums in the organisation to give them visibility and also to establish them in their new roles. He had worked out a new structure that would involve them both. His son would be the National Head of Commercial Development and his daughter would be the National Head of Residential Development. That way, he felt he would have both his key business units covered and when the time came for him to retire, one of them would take over the reins of the whole organisation. Rajat was now preparing the board and his executive team for his impending departure, but the rest of the company still had no idea about it.

Both his children had big plans for the business and had already started making an impact by 'professionalising' the organisation. They had begun to bring in the new ways of working, technology, and thinking that they had picked up through their education and experience of working in other businesses. Rajat was proud of them and of the company he had built. He was now looking forward to planning his retirement over the coming years, knowing his company was in safe hands.

However, today, six months into this transition period, as he watched the dark clouds roll in, he couldn't help but wonder what he had missed when he started the succession process. The organisation was now in turmoil. Some of his senior leaders had quit the business a few months after the announcements. His son was struggling to cope in his new role and was constantly being undermined by his direct reports. Often, they would bypass him and come to Rajat for decisions to be made. His executive team could not seem to make a decision when they got together for their monthly meetings and Rajat found himself constantly stepping in to mediate conflicts. His daughter had started an internal campaign to launch a hospitality business, which he believed was a distraction from their primary strategic objectives.

He reflected on how quickly things had changed in the business. He questioned his decision to appoint his children in key positions as a part of the succession arrangements. He couldn't make sense of the current circumstances. He had thought through a well-executed plan; there was a clear strategic direction for the organisation and a suitable structure and operating model were put in place (at great expense), yet there seemed to be grit in the system that was derailing the process. He considered how he was incentivising his people, whether the governance process worked, and whether he had made the right decision to re-think the operating model. Rajat couldn't get his head around what was going wrong in his organisation, but he knew that something was fundamentally awry, and it could not carry on in this way.

Rajat's story is one of numerous accounts from CEOs and senior leaders that we—the authors of this book—have heard and worked with in our careers. As consultants to organisations of various sizes and complexities, we have been privy to some interesting conundrums and have been asked some challenging consulting questions. Over the years we have worked with CEOs and their executive teams, and HRDs (human resources directors) and their teams, in multiple organisational contexts. Even though our experiences are diverse, we realised very quickly that we have the same approach and use similar models and lenses to approach organisational problems.

The modern narrative has become very much about the individual and individual behaviours. Our economic system, and the rise of the neo-liberal economic discourse more specifically, has driven this. With the individual at the centre of this discourse, little attention is given to the wider ecosystem that the person functions within or how the ecosystem might in fact create the individual. The British psychologist Winnicott famously said, 'There is no such thing as a baby', meaning we never really only ever see a baby, but rather an infant in relationship with its primary caregiver. Humans are always in a relationship and our brains are wired relationally. As opposed to the idea that we are born alone and we die alone, we are in fact born in a relationship and die in a relationship.

In our view, whilst understanding the role of the individual is important, it reveals only a part of the picture. As consultants, we conduct our work in organisations within a different discourse. We are interested in what happens within organisations: we focus on individual and group dynamics. The different types of processes we observe include:

1. intrapersonal/intrapsychic—dynamics within an individual;
2. interpersonal—dynamics between individuals;
3. group-as-a-whole—dynamics happening within the group;
4. intergroup—dynamics between groups;
5. inter-organisational—dynamics between organisations;
6. societal—dynamics in society.

Let us use the iceberg as a metaphor for understanding organisations, one that has been used multiple times by many authors but is still relevant and useful. It was first used by Freud in his famous topographical model. You have probably heard the statistic that approximately 90 per cent of an iceberg is found under water. What is also really interesting is that the bottom of an iceberg houses a unique and dynamic ecosystem. On the surface, icebergs may appear sterile and lifeless, but that's far from the full picture. Ice algae may grow on the underside of an iceberg and these play an important role in creating a flourishing marine ecosystem.

Above the waterline are the tangible parts of the organisation. When we walk into an organisation, what do we see? We see the infrastructure, we see the people, we hear about the policies and procedures; often we see the espoused company values on posters or coffee mugs. These are artefacts of the organisation that are easily accessible.

Below the waterline are the intangibles, the parts that are unseen and take a lot longer to grasp. These are things such as underlying conflicts, power structures, politics, personal agendas, and individual ambition. We have facilitated numerous executive meetings where decisions were made formally in the meeting but then unravelled as soon as the participants left the room and gathered around the water cooler. This was no different in Rajat's business.

The problem that he wanted us to work with was how to help him move this business forward. What we were concerned with was whether he had identified the problem accurately as we were still struggling to put our fingers on what the 'real' issue was. The big challenge in consultancy is slowing down and asking the right questions before jumping in to solve the immediate problem. It is not our job to respond quickly to the client's need to reduce the anxiety of the problem. Instead, it is to help them, as one of our clients says, 'hold the problem a little longer', in order to truly understand the root causes. We have come to realise that the process of inquiry is in itself an intervention. Often, we frustrate our clients by constantly getting them to question 'what is happening above and below the surface' and also 'why they think this is happening'. This process helps to unpack the complexity of the organisational issue.

Before embarking on this project, Rajat invited us to a breakfast meeting at the Taj Mahal Hotel in Mumbai. We sat at the Apollo Bar overlooking the famous Gateway of India and he began telling us his story and describing what he thought the problem was. He started outlining what he wanted us to do and creating a roadmap for the project. We slowed him down, and we asked him a question that he later said no one had ever asked him on before. That makes sense, he was the patriarch—why should he be questioned about his decisions?

All we asked him was: 'Do you want to leave this business?'

His immediate response was: 'Yes, I think the next generation need to lead this business.'

We pushed him again: 'Forgive us, but we are asking you a different question: do you want to leave and retire from this business?'

At which point he sat back, took a deep breath and closed his eyes. The silence only lasted a few seconds, but we knew that we had probably touched something. He opened his eyes and said, 'I don't want to, but I think I need to. It's the only way the next generation can be successful.'

We spent the rest of the morning letting him talk and working through what this all meant for him and for the future of his business.

Consultants' reflections

In planning the future of his organisation, Rajat had paid a lot of attention to the tangible—the top of iceberg—components. He had ensured his children had got the right education and capability; he had put in place the operating model and structure required for the business to function. However, whilst he had focused on setting up the structure, the systems and the strategy, what was missing was a consideration of the intangibles and how they might potentially get in the way of successfully implementing this new phase.

Whilst most organisations have a formal structure, a lot of decision-making and 'work' ends up being done in the white spaces. Relationships can help block or unblock routes of communication and decision-making in organisations. Studies by pioneering researcher Karen Stephenson found how informal organisational networks based on trust could work directly against the espoused hierarchy. The informal organisation is a powerful one and stays hidden below the surface. We have seen far too many organisations where the most powerful person in the organisation is the personal assistant to the CEO. This is because he or she is the individual who controls all the information that goes in or out of the CEO's office and who, most importantly, controls access to the CEO.

We have worked in many organisations where there have been clear procedures or policies for getting work done. However, by working through the informal organisation, some people are able to bypass these policies and get what they need faster than others. Take a look at any of the big fraud cases: whilst all those organisations involved had strict and clear policies, rogue individuals circumvented them to their advantage. In Rajat's situation, this was amplified. The informal organisation was overpowering the formal. Governance and structural codes were being overridden by personal relationships. Those who had a relationship with Rajat were using their currency to bypass his children and go to him directly for decisions. And Rajat in turn was inadvertently fuelling this by not pushing back or sending them to his children instead. He was unable to see his part in perpetuating the problem and thought that the problem lay with loose governance and control procedures.

From this, we can see that the human system dynamics really sit below the iceberg and for leaders in organisations there is a huge imperative to focus on what is going on below the waterline in order to help them deal with the disruptions above the waterline. Even though there is a formal organisation, it is the informal organisation that makes things work. It is the ecosystem that we cannot see that actually runs the organisation. And this ecosystem is called the 'culture' of the organisation.

One of the best definitions of culture we have come across is by Edgar Schein, who says that culture is: 'A pattern of **shared basic assumptions** that the group learned as it solved its problems of **external adaptation** *and **internal integration**, that has worked well enough to be considered valid and, therefore, to be taught to new members as the correct way to perceive, think, and feel in relation to those problems'* (Schein, 2010)[1]. Let us unpick this definition.

The shared basic assumptions refer to the unconscious patterns of behaviour, the way things are done in an organisation. It helps individuals make sense of the world around them. These basic assumptions determine the organisation's attitudes and therefore its actions. An organisation's culture is ephemeral and intangible, which means it is hard to grasp. However, our role as consultants is to bring these deeply held assumptions in an organisation to the surface in order to intervene effectively. For example, in an organisation where there is a belief that the only way to get ahead is tenure, this assumption will hold back those people who are highly ambitious, as they will believe they will always be trumped by someone with longer service. Consequently, those with high drives and motivation will leave as they cannot see their careers progressing, while others just work away and keep their heads down in order to clock up tenure in order to get promoted. This is not an organisational policy and the CEO will deny this is what happens if asked—but as a deeply held belief, it drives the behaviour in that organisation because this is the reality the staff experience.

The family values that Rajat had put in place were very helpful in driving the business forward but one of the basic assumptions that existed in the organisation was that of a strong patriarch and family hierarchy. You did not question the father figure and he had hitherto guided the business in everything. This meant that there was a dependency on him in a debilitating way. It also meant that this dependency on the patriarch would undermine anyone else trying to take up their own authority or agency. Of course this was happening unawares, as Rajat would say he had put in place the structure and created appropriate roles for others to take charge.

The robustness of the culture will enable an organisation to deal with changes, volatility, and pressures of an external context. This is the idea of external adaptation. For example, a client we worked

---

[1] Schein, E. H. (2010). *Organizational Culture and Leadership.* San Francisco, CA: Jossey-Bass.

with in financial services managed to ride out the crisis in the UK. They attributed this to their strong culture, which was the guiding light that helped them navigate the trials of a very difficult period in the world economy. They knew that 'what' they did would not necessarily help them through the crisis; but clearly defining 'how' they did it would help their organisation adapt quickly to the external environment. The culture Rajat had built within the business was one of strong family values. And these family values had similarly helped them come together closely over the years to deal with any of the challenges that the markets threw at them.

In terms of internal integration, a strong culture will enable organisations to manage their internal boundaries. A common language, identity, the nature of authority and relationships, and allocation of rewards and status will all determine how people pull together in order to achieve the strategic objectives of the organisation.

The field of OD is wide and there are some practitioners who work entirely on what is tangible and above the surface, while others work only with the material below the surface. As consultants, we are constantly helping leaders and organisations understand how what lies beneath could impact what is above the waterline and vice versa. Dysfunctional organisational dynamics can easily distract an organisation from its strategic objectives. Often, we find that leaders ignore some of these dynamics by tackling the problem with above-the-waterline solutions. At the same time, we need to be cognisant that businesses and organisations have to focus on building a robust, visible, and commercial organisation. A sudden change in strategy impacts the emotional life of the organisation as well. There is a fallacy that OD work deals with the 'soft stuff'. In our view, when taking into account a whole organisational system, we need to consider both the business imperatives and the organisational dynamics to make impactful and sustainable interventions. In other words, we need to look at and work with the entire iceberg.

One of the biggest problems that organisations face is jumping quickly to solution mode. As human beings, we get anxious when we have a problem. This anxiety leads us to search for a solution to reduce our anxiety, rather than one to solve the actual problem. It becomes more about the problem of having a problem rather than the problem itself.

Rajat's initial request was for us to review whether the structure was fit for purpose and where the loose ends were in terms of the organisational design that he wanted to implement. The problem, in his mind, was structural and, by creating good governance process, he believed this would solve the behaviours that he was witnessing.

What next?

Rajat's inability to let go was being mirrored by the rest of the organisation in their dependency on him and their subsequent reluctance to let him go. Whilst Rajat was creating new operating models and structures, there were dynamics brewing beneath the surface that were derailing his plans. And somehow, unconsciously, he was self-sabotaging this, as he was unable to leave what was essentially his creation, his baby and his life.

This set the tone for a very different type of engagement. It was not about governance or structure but more about ensuring a space could be created to enable the organisation to work with transitions. The loss of a parent is significant, and this made it very difficult for the organisational system. We helped the business over the next eighteen months to work with this transition. We created spaces where the leadership team could envision what the future would look like with a new CEO, Rajat's son. We supported Rajat's son in establishing what his rules of engagement would be and his expectations from his executive team. We worked with both his son and daughter to set them up as a strong pair who would lead this business.

We helped Rajat take a backseat and accept a non-executive role on the board from which he could mentor the next generation. This also meant that the shock of loss was not great for the organisation, as he was still around. Creating the boundary between Rajat and his children was important as they started to be seen as the driving force in the organisation, while he became one of the respected elders in the family who could advise but who would not be critical to delivery. This enabled him to retain a position within the family, and it helped the organisation deal with the transition to the new generation. It enabled the new generation to take up their own agency and run the business, while having access to and being guided by their elders.

The focus of the work on this project became about supporting the transitions in the organisation, of which there were multiple: Rajat to his new role, his children into leadership positions, the organisation into accepting both the new leadership and Rajat's new role, and also the interpersonal relationships between Rajat and his children. What we were particularly in tune with was not 'killing off' the patriarch or replacing him with a new one. It was about enabling a new, next generation of leaders to emerge and take up their authority in their own way. And for the organisation to move into its next phase of development.

As you read the stories in this book, we urge you to question what is going on behind what is initially presented in the client problems. We invite you to form hypotheses about these as you consider both the stories and the consultants' reflections. Often you may disagree with these reflections and have your own ideas, based on your understanding of the story. This highlights the relational aspect of this work and what goes on in between the events of a story and the different players, both within and outside the narrative. We hope this will help you to engage in a different, richer line of enquiry to truly get to what lies beneath.

2. London

We played phone tag for a few days. Text messages and voicemails were exchanged with little hope of us actually speaking. Natalia was trying hard to get in touch with me (Ajit), but for some reason we kept missing each other. She was the human resources director (HRD) of a private bank in London. We finally pinned each other down and she told me her story.

The bank had a history of over a hundred years, she explained. As a part of a new strategic initiative, she had been hired to reinvigorate the HR function and the bank's approach to their people. She wanted help to design a new people strategy; a strategic vision and plan for how the organisation was going to engage with their people. This would incorporate everything from hiring to learning and reward.

My colleague James and I went to visit Natalia and the CEO for an initial meeting. Their offices were located in an old and beautiful building near the Bank of England, right in the heart of the City of London. The lobby was plush but understated. It was unlike any of the big modern buildings just a stone's throw away. There was beautiful artwork in the lobby and there hung two portraits of the founders. There was a strong sense of history about this organisation.

The story of the founders and the business was written on the walls along the corridors.

We were ushered into a meeting room where we met Natalia and the CEO, Juliette. Natalia was spritely, in her mid-forties and full of enthusiasm. Juliette, in her mid-sixties, on the other hand, was more reserved. She spent most of the meeting listening whilst Natalia did most of the talking.

I was struck by the language Natalia used: 'You come highly recommended to me so I am hopeful that you will be able to help me,' she said. She kept mentioning that she wanted to change what existed currently as she did not think it was fit for purpose. When I asked her why, she could not articulate what she thought was specifically wrong. She was unable to express what problem the new people strategy would fix. I asked her whether she thought it would be useful for us to work with her to understand the nature and size of the problem first, before we went on to design any solutions. I explained that this might help us focus our efforts and have the impact she desired. She seemed relieved at my suggestion and commissioned us to do a preliminary diagnostic of the organisation.

I asked Juliette what she thought of this and she agreed that this was the right approach, although she still seemed very distant. I put this down to it being our first meeting and our not having formed a relationship yet. She asked us what we would do and how the process would work. I outlined a design for the diagnostic process. We would conduct individual interviews with the senior executive team and a number of cross-hierarchy and departmental focus groups with the staff. We would also conduct observations on the floor and review their existing people processes. The purpose was to understand the existing culture and ways of working at the bank, current issues and their root causes, and to gather suggestions for improvement. This would help us build an appropriate people strategy for them. Natalia and Juliette said that they would run this by the executive team and confirm with us later in the day.

James and I left feeling enthusiastic and reflected on how exciting this engagement could be. Later that afternoon Natalia called me to say that the plan was received with great enthusiasm by the executive team, who were keen for us to get started.

The diagnostic process

During her interview, Juliette seemed fatigued. Her responses were defensive, and she was dismissive of any issues we raised with the solutions that she had apparently put in place. She repeatedly suggested that she had done everything she could for the organisation and that her staff were not taking up the opportunities she was offering them. In her mind, she and the executive team had created an open environment. The blame for the issues lay with the way the staff were responding. She also blamed the previous HRD for her dogmatic views and processes, which did not help in enabling an open environment. She said that she was at her wits' end and that she was very happy we had come on board to help her and the executive team.

The executive team were not very complimentary of Juliette and her leadership style. They felt that she had 'checked out' and lacked energy. They believed they needed new leadership. Some of the interviewees were disparaging of Juliette's capabilities, saying that the organisation needed a new visionary leader to lead them. They felt that bringing in Natalia was a good move as she was already shaking up some of the old ways of working. They were concerned that if the bank were to survive another 100 years, it would need fresh energy to take them there.

To access some of the underlying narrative in the organisation, we used a creative methodology in the focus groups. The groups were given a set of postcards and were asked to pick those that described their experience in the organisation.

In the first group, the responses were extremely brief and guarded and we could feel the resistance. About thirty minutes into the second focus group I made an intervention that opened up the discussion. I said, 'I wonder how you are feeling about being here.' This led to a variety of responses but the strongest feeling in the room was one of despair and hopelessness. The group said they felt as though they were going through the motions of giving feedback while knowing very clearly that nothing would change. They felt that over the past few years they had been battered and abused with the amount of criticism they had received from the external world and they felt abandoned by their leadership.

The executive team had a high turnover (except for the CEO) and every time issues were raised; yet no change came from it. They had become used to a lack of decision-making at senior levels and did not know who to go to for what. This constant change, they said, had left them anxious. They were unable to trust whether the executive team were there to truly support them or to further their own agendas. Especially since many of the executives were on interim contracts, there was a feeling that they would only pursue short-term goals in order to make a mark before their contracts ended. Staff felt that there was no clear direction or strategy for the organisation and that they were in a 'rudderless ship'. They felt that the leaders were absent and not available.

We asked the focus groups why they stayed if things were so bad, and the response surprised us. We learned that the organisation had a high turnover at all levels and many people would stay for a short time and use the brand on their CV to move on.

Presenting the results

When we presented our results to the executive and the CEO they were accepting and not resistant. To our surprise, we then learned that there had been an investigation into the organisation's performance by an independent body, which had been critical of it. It had pointed out a number of deficiencies similar to what we had found in the organisation. We had not heard about this before and were surprised that both the CEO and the HRD had failed to mention it to us.

When I asked them why this had not been mentioned before, Juliette, the CEO, became visibly upset. She said that she was tired of being constantly blamed for what was going on. She stated that she didn't understand what more she could do for the organisation. Instead of defending the results, we (the consulting team) stayed curious and nurturing, and asked her how she felt, based on what she was hearing. She said she was disappointed and deflated, and looked to me to suggest a solution.

I resisted this and stayed with the experience in the room. We explored more of what was going on for them and processed how it felt for the executive team to hear the feedback. We then co-created an intervention plan where the team brainstormed solutions and interventions rather than me providing them with the answers.

The meeting ended positively and Natalia, the HRD, later thanked us for our work and help. She asked us to put together a commercial contract for the next steps of work for approval by the board.

What next?

A week after we submitted our proposal, the board of the organisation announced that due to various factors they had to downsize and a number of cuts would be made at all levels. The organisation would be significantly reduced over a period of two years.

Natalia called me in a panic and said, 'Everyone is very upset and shocked. We had given them some hope by starting the transition process; however, this changes everything and reinforces that we are not valued and the work that we are doing is not seen to be important.'

She said that the executive team had decided to run an all-staff awayday where they wanted to energise the staff in light of the terrible news. They wanted to motivate staff to keep working over the next two years as they wound down the organisation.

The bank were looking to me to rescue them by running the awayday. If I agreed with them, I would end up colluding with the situation. I declined and explained to them that the organisation was in shock, and questioned if a motivating event was the right intervention. I spoke to them about transitions and I engaged them in a conversation about what they were losing and what they were gaining through this process of change. They heard me out, reluctantly. Natalia supported my thinking and agreed that we had to attend to the main anxiety: the impending winding down of the business.

The others insisted that we put together a design for an awayday for them so they could have something to serve as a comparison when they spoke to other providers. I felt that if we ran an event that did not acknowledge the pain of the current situation, we would once again end up reinforcing the dynamics of the past, whereby staff raised issues and were not heard by management. I thought this would be a good opportunity to provide a space for some healing in the relationship instead and that together they could deal with the tumultuous times ahead.

We designed an awayday which was based on dialogue and conversation. Through the use of creative social dialogue activity, we would create an environment where they could engage in a conversation about their current circumstances and envision a new future for themselves. Natalia loved the design and put it forward to the executive team, who were in agreement with the plan.

The day before the staff awayday I was taken severely ill and was admitted into hospital for an emergency operation. I was anxious for the organisation, but I knew that my best and most experienced consultants were on the job.

I learned afterwards that Juliette, the CEO, arrived late on the day and then left after only an hour. The group noticed this and were very angry, voicing their upset throughout the discussions. They felt abandoned by the organisation and now by Juliette, who had not been present for the day. The consultants helped the group process what was going on for them and to build a picture of what the future might look like. The consultant team felt that, though difficult, it was a useful day as finally the organisation was engaging in an open dialogue.

Consultant's reflections

From the very beginning, I felt the group was according me a leadership role through their overwhelming positive responses to my suggestions, the speed of contracting, commissioning, and the acceptance of everything I said at face value. I knew that I have a tendency to 'rescue' and when subjected to these dynamics this was activated in me. I used this insight; if they were looking to me to lead this group, I felt I could use it to mobilise the process and start the work. This served me well up to a point; I had been able to play the role of a leader and quickly mobilise the diagnostic process.

However, I wondered if helping them with the awayday was a mistake on my part. I gave them what they wanted by playing into their dependency needs. I got caught up in the moment, ignored my previous awareness of the dynamic and ended up attempting to rescue them. I felt it was a deviation from my original task. I was there to support the organisation on their strategic journey. Instead, I ended up designing and running an awayday, which contaminated my working relationship with the client.

Supervision conversation

Trevor: My first question is: what was the problem they were trying to solve? You say you were asked to design a people strategy, but what was the problem and why was this the solution? I am wondering what Natalia really wanted.

Ajit: Well, I was told that as she was new to the organisation, she had been given the mandate to build the people strategy. Hence, in her view, a coherent people strategy—which was currently missing—would be a starting point for her.

Trevor: So, you followed her lead. Do you think you really understood what the problem was?

Ajit: As I couldn't get a fix on the problem, the diagnostic process was intended to help with this.

Trevor: All right, another line of questioning: did she recruit you or your consulting team?

Ajit: In hindsight, I think the above-the-surface answer would be that she recruited the team, as there were three of us working on the job. However, what she did do was to call me and refer to a prior piece of work and talk about how I came to her highly recommended. So, the below-the-surface answer would be that she intended to recruit me.

Trevor: I wonder if seduction was your entry into this system. The first thing she says to you is that 'you' come so highly recommended, not your business. What did this trigger for you? How did you unconsciously respond to this? This could have set up a triangulated relationship between you, Natalia, and Juliette. I am intrigued about your own relationship to triangulated relationships. You say you have a propensity to be drawn into the role of rescuer and caretaker. Could it be that you have taken on the role of rescuing the HRD whilst at some level setting up an antagonistic relationship with the CEO?

Ajit: Hold on, my route into the organisation was the HRD. She was the primary client and I was working for her.

Trevor: Again, you are speaking about 'I'. What about the rest of your team?

Ajit: Now, come to think of it, my team was also made up of three people. There was me, my colleague, and an associate who joined us in a temporary capacity.

Trevor: If we go with the line of seduction, Natalia already knew what was going to come out of your report, based on the previous assessment. She didn't tell you that this had been conducted. In some way, she recruited you to collude with her to present a similar finding to Juliette. You played into this seduction and perhaps also ended up shaming Juliette.

Ajit: Your pointing out the seduction makes me feel ashamed of my approach. How could I not have seen this? I have played into the process and have become part of the organisational dysfunction.

Trevor: Falling for seduction is truly human and is part of the consulting process. The role of a process consultant is extremely complex when it comes to contracting and working with an organisational client. Being valued for your input is seductive, both personally as well as financially. My pointing out the seduction to you makes you feel ashamed. By pointing this out to you, how quickly have I shamed you ... So, think about what the parallel process was with the CEO.

Ajit: I can see how I perhaps played into something there in the first part of this engagement. However, I am still quite confused about the second bit and the awayday.

Trevor: The trap of acquiescing to the client's wants rather than needs is ever present. However, so is the danger of being thrown out by the system for not doing so. It is a fine line to carry some of the projections of the system, both positive and negative, and to not simultaneously collude [with the system]. Additionally, when there is dynamic of dependency playing out and you take up the baton to rescue the group from the anxiety-provoking situation, a perfect storm has been created.

Ajit: Makes sense now ... From when the HRD first called me for help, the executive team's request for a solution, and then finally being unconsciously manoeuvred into running the awayday, I was being pulled into a position of a dependent leader by the group. I was set up as a saviour, as someone who could solve the difficulties of the executive team. In not wanting to persecute the client by resisting the awayday, I set myself up for a fall. I ended up colluding with the executive team and taking on a leadership role that was unconsciously assigned to me. If the new leader takes up that role, they are usually set up and end up in the same place as the old leader. I had initially maintained my boundaries and was aware of the process. However, the seduction of helping the client was so strong that I ended up succumbing to the dynamic.

Trevor: Yes, and the awayday turned out to be an opportunity for Juliette to unconsciously shame you and discredit the process. You have recognised that you strayed away from what you were initially asked to do. The seduction pushed you into the task and did not create the space for you to process what was going on. You knew that the awayday was not appropriate, and you tried to make the best of a bad situation. However, I am left thinking whether you actually unconsciously knew this would not work. You fell ill and the CEO sabotaged the process, ultimately killing you and the consulting team off.

I think you were already in a double bind. If you had refused to do the awayday, my hypothesis is that the CEO would have found another way to kill you off. The system ejected you and closed their boundaries; hence you have not heard from them and also not from the HRD.

The question I want to leave you with is this: to what extent did the propensity to rescue get in the way of holding a strong boundary with the client? Considering this may help you understand the warning signs of being seduced.

What next?

Following my recovery, I received an email from Natalia saying that I was to go in to speak to the executive team. It felt like I was being asked to report to the headmaster's office for a telling-off. I was filled with anxiety as I walked out of the underground station and made my way to their offices. My colleague and I were met by Natalia at reception. She was tentative and jittery—not her usual enthusiastic self. We were to meet the head of finance, the head of marketing, and herself. They placed us at the end of a long table, facing the three of them.

They felt the event had left the organisation angry and not motivated in the way that they had wanted, and asked us to explain what had happened. They said that if I had been there perhaps the day would have gone differently. I processed this with them, explaining that my best and most experienced consultants were in attendance. What I felt they were actually saying was that they felt let down and abandoned by me on the day.

I said that we achieved what we set out to do. We let people feel heard and seen; we created a space for dialogue and acknowledgement of the feelings of anxiety and uncertainty that the transition would bring. I suggested that any further work should focus around helping the organisation deal with their loss and work through the transition. I asked them if we could collectively think through what the real problem was here and how we could collaboratively solve it.

They were unable to engage in this line of conversation. It felt too anxiety-provoking for them. Instead, they asked us to send through a proposal for their next steps.

I left the room feeling conflicted. I had been called in to discuss why the day had 'failed' in their eyes and then at the end of it they had asked me send in a proposal for the next steps. The act of asking for a proposal seemed to be a defence mechanism that they used whenever they found themselves in a situation they could not solve. They wanted the solution to be presented to them and for someone to implement it on their behalf. It seemed like asking to be rescued again and my colleague and I felt that if we did this, we would end up perpetuating the cycle. I decided not to send them a proposal and instead invited them to an initial workshop to dialogue and co-create a way forward instead.

Since then, despite having followed up many times, I have not heard back from either the executive team or Natalia.

3. Hong Kong

Those butterflies I (Trevor) knew so well began their well-rehearsed trip around my stomach as we descended into Hong Kong. They were an indication of both the complexity of the task at hand, and of my excitement at eating again at my favourite *tonkatsu* restaurant off Nathan Road. The early summer humidity hit me as I walked out of Hong Kong International Airport down the walkway to the taxi rank. 'IFC Mall,' I told the taxi driver. There would be just enough time to grab a coffee from one of the new hip coffee bars in the mall before making my way up to the thirty-fifth floor to meet Jenny and Emma. We had met in these offices many times over the five years I had worked with their organisation, an Australian software development company.

Julia, the office manager, opened the big glass door for me with her usual warm but slightly uncomfortable smile; we still hadn't worked out whether to hug or shake hands. She showed me to the boardroom for my meeting. This trip was to be different as Jenny and Emma had decided their time leading the organisation had come to an end.

The organisation and consulting context

After ten exceptionally successful years, Jenny and Emma were listing their business on the stock exchange and handing over the reins. They had said that the meeting this morning was to ensure that I would be on top of maintaining the culture they had worked so hard to build.

The two founders had met at university and had always talked about one day running a company. Emma had studied economics but had then gone on to do an MBA, before working for a few years in the consulting world. Jenny had studied to become an accountant and had spent a few years at one of the big audit firms. Both had worked with major clients in the financial services sector and had spotted a gap in the market for a digital platform for the banking industry.

Emma had been the ideas person; she was charismatic and a risk taker whilst Jenny had brought reason, financial controls, and process to the business. Emma and Jenny played the good and bad parents with ease, and their partnership was seen as incredibly powerful. They were a mythical couple not just in the organisation, but also in the wider software development community. Together, they provided the balance that had allowed the organisation to grow organically over the decade they had been in business.

They had started the business in the early days of FinTech (Financial Technology). The market conditions in Australia had been kind to them, but unlike many other software development start-ups, they had grown slowly and had been careful not to trade too much of the business for external investment. Jenny had ensured that they kept their overheads and headcount low, and had turned a profit from early on. They had made a big impact in the Australian market before deciding to expand into the Asian and European markets.

Emma had ensured that throughout the expansion process, the underlying culture was maintained and strengthened. She and Jenny had engaged with organisation development (OD) consultants in Australia from early on and had a long-term relationship with a colleague of mine before I got involved with the organisation, following their expansion into the European and Asian market.

The leadership team they had brought on board had focused strongly on sales and had helped to drive strong profits. In particular, Alastair had run the Australian sales team and had seen them grow from strength to strength. He had come from a traditional financial services background and had brought a strong, process-driven mindset into the sales business unit. He was seen as highly efficient and pragmatic, and was the natural choice to run the global sales team. The only concern was that where Emma was charismatic and engaging, Alastair was seen as clinical and a strong taskmaster.

Emma had brought me on board in order to ensure that the culture was maintained as they expanded into new markets, understanding that this would not be Alastair's focus. Therefore, my role had been to provide leadership development programmes for up-and-coming leaders, and through these to ensure the continued strength of the culture. Unlike most of our contracts, where we consult as a team, the organisation insisted that only I was required on this contract. I had tried to push back here but to no avail.

The consulting process

It was an ongoing joke in the organisation that OD was there as the 'culture police', to ensure that everyone had drunk the cultural 'Kool-Aid'. Yet despite such disparaging jokes about 'culture', it was the one thing everyone consistently spoke about. And it was culture that, in my experience, kept engagement levels high during tough times …

I was contracted to provide five days of consulting services per month to the company in their Dublin and Hong Kong offices, and a further two days in Sydney. Whilst keeping to those numbers of days in Hong Kong and Sydney was easy to do, working with the Dublin office was a different story. It was my girlfriend who first brought this to my attention, asking me exactly how much extra I was working with this client. I was taking phone calls every day and doing Skype calls with them most evenings. I rationalised it at first as being necessary to build the relationship, but, slowly, I had to acknowledge that something else was at play.

I am generally good at holding boundaries around contracts with my clients; being a therapist in practice has trained me well. With this client, I was being pulled more and more into being part of the organisation. I even began talking about 'us' as if I were a member of staff.

According to the stance I take as a consultant, I position myself as being neither 'in' the organisation as a full-time employee would be, nor 'out' of the organisation as consultants who provide one-off pieces of work might be. I see one of my strengths as being able to place myself close enough to organisations to understand their culture well, but simultaneously outside of them to the degree that I am not pulled into their internal politics. This is referred to as being 'on' the organisation's boundary. On this occasion, I had to acknowledge that I had been drawn in by the culture and was functioning 'in' the organisation.

Alastair was based in Dublin, and I noticed that my conversations with him had changed from consulting conversations about what was happening within the organisation, to being given instructions as to what he would like me to do in the organisation. Even though I had become aware of what was happening, I was not that invested in changing anything. I had become very attached to the organisation and felt included in it and part of it. This was in stark contrast to my usual manner—which was not really wanting to become part of any organ- isation. I usually really loved being a consultant and hovering on the edges, yet something was different for me in this company.

I began to realise that I had become Emma's proxy in terms of safeguarding the organisational culture in Asia and in Europe, where Alastair spent most of his time. She wanted me there as she understood that Alastair would not keep track of what was happening culturally.

Alastair and I had a very transactional relationship. It always felt like he tolerated my presence and wished for me to be more pragmatic and less focused on what was happening under the surface in the organisation. However, we kept in our own lanes and played to our strengths.

Alastair had done a really great job in expanding the business globally, especially in Europe. He had built a strong sales team and gained much respect internally and in the wider market. However, what I found concerning was that there was a big leadership gap between him and those below him. He was aware of this but held on to the fantasy that it could be solved, if only the recruitment team could find him strong leaders 'out there' in the market. My initial attempts to make it clearer to him that the leadership gap was possibly a reflection of what was going on inside the organisation—and related to team and organisation dynamics—brought on strong defensive reactions from him. However, I soon found myself colluding and stopped providing interpretations that triggered his defences.

The leadership gap meant that thinking about the business was done by Alastair, while the rest of the employees in the Dublin office had become experts in task delivery. This was not that different from the Australian office, in that the founders ensured they were involved in making and signing off all the financial decisions and were intimately involved in the day-to-day running of the whole organisation. The leadership trio's energy and ability to keep track of all the detail by was, to say the least, impressive. However, they were also looked up to and spoken about in unrealistic ways by the rest of the organisation.

What continually concerned me was the sustainability of the organisation under their leadership and the lack of any real succession planning. Alastair had always been seen as the natural successor to Emma and Jenny, but someone who would lead the organisation in a very different way. Questions were always asked about his ability to engage hearts and minds, and how he would ever replace Emma and Jenny.

The listing

The possibility of a listing had always been spoken about, and there was a lot of excitement when it was announced. With the expansion in Asia having been so successful, it was decided that they would list the business on the Hong Kong stock exchange. The year leading up to the listing was extremely busy and consultants were brought in to assist with preparing for life as a listed company.

Internally, questions were asked about how Emma and Jenny would respond to the continual scrutiny that would accompany the listing. Like many business founders, they enjoyed the freedom that came from growing a start-up. Founders tend to struggle with the continual interrogation that comes from shareholders, analysts, and industry regulators. Talk around the water cooler was about whether Alastair might be the right person, owing to his preference for process and procedure. So, a few months after the listing took place, it wasn't a complete surprise when Emma and Jenny announced that they would be stepping into non-executive positions, and that Alastair would be taking up the CEO position. He would also be appointing a new Chief Financial Officer (CFO) from one of the Asian banks.

The handover took around six months, and it was interesting how quickly things changed. There were a number of changes in organisational structure as well as in the make-up of the senior leadership team (SLT). The share price remained strong, as were the first and second quarter results, but the conversations people in the organisation had with me changed in content and quality.

Anxiety in the system

Where there had been optimism and energetic engagement, now there was cynicism and a loss of energy. Some of the conversations were quite depressing and I became aware of how, suddenly, I was holding my boundaries around my time commitments much more clearly. I often felt tired and emotionally drained.

The organisation had always had a strong commitment to the health and wellbeing of its employees and was well known in the industry for its innovative wellness programme. As a clinical psychologist, I was asked periodically to have conversations with staff members who were experiencing mental health difficulties, and to refer them on to external clinicians and psychotherapists when necessary. It was during this time of change that I noticed a sharp increase in the number of people who approached me with increased symptoms of anxiety. What was interesting was that many of those I spoke to had never experienced anxiety before. I had even noticed an increase in my own anxiety when working in the organisation's different offices.

That morning in Hong Kong, the increase in anxiety took up a fair portion of our conversation. What I received in response was not unexpected. Though empathetic to people's experiences, the suggested solution was to increase care for those individuals experiencing symptoms. The idea that this problem was systemic found no resonance with either Emma or Jenny.

The conversation shifted to my concerns about the abrupt change in culture since the listing. Again, whilst being understanding, they felt that they needed to leave Alastair to run the organisation the way in which he saw fit. They further said that looking after the culture was my role and that they trusted me to do this. It felt to me that my role as consultant to the business was no longer the main reason I was there, and that I might as well be employed full-time.

My work in the organisation continued somewhat precariously. Whilst I knew that I had a responsibility to work with what was happening beneath the surface, I was aware that the new style of leadership was more inclined to want traditional management consulting than the consulting type of OD I work with. I believed that the consulting position was important to ensure the continued success of the organisation and to assist the change in developmental stages. How to do this without raising defences was my dilemma.

Consultant's reflections

My first reflection was why the organisation hired me as an individual rather than as part of the usual consulting pair. I thought another pair would have been too difficult for the organisation and would have undermined Alastair. I was left wondering whether or not Alastair had been unconsciously chosen as Jenny's replacement, and if I was therefore seen as a replacement for Emma's more psychological role.

A further hypothesis was that the power of the parental pair—that is, of Emma and Jenny—had left the entire system developmentally unready to leave their metaphoric 'childhood' and move into a more adult state. Alastair did not challenge the founders' legacy, as his style was far more transactional and provided little in terms of cultural perpetuation.

This led to another hypothesis regarding the heightened levels of anxiety in the system. The powerful pairing of Emma and Jenny had provided containment of anxiety. The belief in the omnipotence of the mythical 'parents' had left the 'children' feeling safe. When Emma and Jenny moved aside, the rest of the organisation no longer felt safe. Alastair was too pragmatic and emotionally unresponsive to take on this role, which meant the organisation had been restructured in a way that it was not developmentally ready for. They were unprepared for the 'parents' to leave, and how this would impact the ongoing performance of the organisation concerned me.

The feeling I was left with resembled being in a relationship where love has died and what is left is a slightly depressing transactional arrangement.

Supervision conversation

Ajit: You speak a lot about the powerful pair of Emma and Jenny through your work with the client, and how their leaving has impacted the entire organisation. You also reflect a lot on how you feel that you have had to take on much of what they did for the organisation, thereby pulling you out of your role as a consultant. I am really curious about the role you usually take up in groups. Can you reflect upon where you usually find yourself in a group?

Trevor: Wow, that is an interesting thing to ponder on! I suppose my usual position is to become the advocate or protector for the group. I will take on fights for them and happily become the bad one in the group. I will generally point out things that no one else will say. But I would say that my primary position in groups is to be the caretaker of the members.

Ajit: So, let's take this back a bit. You were pulled out of your consulting team and recruited by the organisation as a single consultant. It feels to me like you were seduced by the group into taking on a role on behalf of the organisation. I wonder if you would have acted or showed up differently if you were in a consulting pair.

Trevor: My usual style is to function independently as a 'lone wolf'. It's something I know well and pairing is not my natural position. So, the client gave me an out from my consulting pair and allowed me to take up a more comfortable and perhaps not helpful position.

Ajit: Yes, that is what I am reflecting on as well. What did the organisation achieve by breaking up the consulting pair and what role did they actually recruit you for?

Trevor: What I am thinking about now is that the organisation is not ready for Emma and Jenny to leave. Having me as their proxy, and for me to take on a conflictual relationship with Alastair, means that the organisation does not do the work of really moving on from the founding 'parents'. I am in fact reinforcing the organisation's problems.

Ajit: It feels as if you have been co-opted and have colluded with the needs of the organisation. You have become the rescuer for the wider system. For example, you start off this case by saying you were recruited to provide leadership development. You never speak of this and very quickly start talking about how you were involved in building the culture or furthermore engaging almost as a therapist with the organisation. This has blurred the boundaries of your role as an OD consultant, working with the organisation providing systemic feedback. They have attempted to pull you inside even though you still remain a consultant in title. So, from your reflection, this is what you usually do in groups. What I mean is, you do end up being the person who takes up the fight on the group's behalf.

Trevor: As I think through this, this is a role I have always taken on since childhood. I did it at school, I did it throughout university, and I find myself doing this within my circle of friends. It's like I feel compelled to point out things that are wrong for the group but that the group will not speak about. This was perfect growing up in South Africa, as I became the 'white person' who would say the things that others were thinking and feeling but were not willing to say. In most instances, the group ends up giving me a badge of honour.

Ajit: However, it does multiple things which may or may not be helpful for you as a consultant to groups and organisations. First, you are unable to then be on the boundary and provide the group with feedback. Instead, you join the group and fight the aggressor. If you turn around and question the group or provide them with feedback—which is your role as a consultant—you will very quickly become a persecutor and be ejected from the system. Second, this keeps you safe. What I mean is, it guarantees your position in the group.

Trevor: Wait, what you are saying is that my role of consultant is not that of an activist? I'm now recognising that I get a lot from the group by taking up this role, but in fact it keeps the group in a state of dependency. That really does make sense to me, and helps to explain my experience of tiredness as well as feeling unable to hold my boundaries on so many levels. I guess the tiredness comes with looking after the feelings of people for the organisation. With Jenny and more especially Emma exiting the organisation, and without the entire system stepping out of its dependency state, someone needs to take on their 'human' role. It's not really that surprising how much more clinical work has come my way since the listing. I feel embarrassed now, thinking about what role I played in this. It makes real sense why I constantly used the term 'us', as if I were part of the organisation. I was made to feel welcome and developed a strong attachment to the organisation. It also makes sense why Alastair was not engaging in OD systemic conversations with me.

Ajit: I'm interested that you say 'embarrassed'; I wonder if your embarrassment comes from the realisation that you have played into the organisational dynamics? It is very difficult not to get pulled into such dynamics when you work alone. I wonder whether the organisation did not desire a strong external consulting pair to come in to replace Emma and Jenny. Rather, it needed someone to hold the anxiety of Emma and Jenny's imminent departure. And that's why they hired you as an individual.

Trevor: That makes real sense. On the surface, it felt very uncomfortable consulting on my own, but now I realise that it played into my own process. It makes me realise how important it is for me to move away from the role of activist and back onto the boundary of being a consultant to the system. What's really interesting, looking back, is a conversation Emma had with me just prior to her leaving, about whether I would ever consider joining the organisation full-time. I must say I was flattered but quickly dismissed the idea, saying I'm not really a good insider. What is also really interesting for me is that I have put off coming to this supervision session for a long time. Perhaps I really wanted to keep my head in the sand rather than give up my position.

Ajit: I cannot tell you how often I have heard the story of the consultant who was approached to move inside the organisation. It is not always the worst option for the organisation or the consultant; however, both need to understand what the role change really means. Being inside is fundamentally different.

Trevor: From this conversation I have realised that my role within the organisation has become completely blurred. I have been drawn in by the organisation and my own desires, and have played into the dynamics of the organisation. What I think I need to do now is to reframe my role. I need to have a conversation about what I will and will not engage in. I cannot be the organisation's consultant, therapist, and activist. The role I signed up for is consultant. This means I need to have the authority in my role to challenge all parts of the system in service of the organisation. And this may mean helping the organisation with the painful transition of leadership and not fighting against the new leader.

Ajit: I agree that is going to be needed. What is going to be difficult but imperative for you is to stand next to the organisation whilst it goes through loss rather than to try to alleviate the pain it may feel. At the same time, you may need to be more aware of signals when you are being seduced to collude with the process.

What next?

Those familiar butterflies began their dance as I descended into Chek Lap Kok airport. The prospect of dining later on fresh sea urchin flown in from Tokyo was one of the reasons. However, that morning's breakfast meeting with Emma, Jenny and Alastair was the main cause. I had set up this meeting to look at what I had been working on over the preceding few months and to report back on my progress. I had purposely decided to ask Emma and Jenny to join us, even though they were now in non-exec roles.

I had decided to build upon what had transpired in the supervision and attempt to regain my consulting position. The decision to have this breakfast meeting instead of meeting in the office was my first step in attempting to redefine my relationship with the organisation. That— and the possibility of fresh dim sum.

We went through the usual pleasantries and small talk before I started on my feedback. Emma quickly jumped in and shared how happy people were with how I was looking after them. Though it felt good to hear this, I saw it as my 'in'. I carefully enquired whether my primary role as an OD consultant hadn't been lost and if I was now functioning rather as the organisation's psychologist. Emma and Jenny both felt that though this was partly true, they had no problem with it. In their mind, I was providing an important service to the organisation and they wanted me to continue doing so. Alastair was less convinced that what they were paying me was justifiable if I was in fact the in-house therapist. We were able to have a really good discussion about whether the organisation really wanted an OD consultant at this point in time. Whilst Emma and Jenny believed that OD consulting was really important, they felt that they needed to allow Alastair to make the decision. He thought that he could run with things on his own for the time being but would call me if and when he felt necessary. We also agreed that utilising me as a psychologist was not cost-effective and this allowed me to refer them to a colleague who ran an employee wellness company out of the Asia-Pacific region.

The outcome of the breakfast meeting was bittersweet. On the one hand, I was walking away from a contract that I really enjoyed. On the other, the meeting ended with an agreement to reconvene at the Tsim Sha Tsui Ferry Pier at 8 p.m. Sea urchin and *tonkatsu* were to be a great reward.

Two years later, I had just finished dinner with colleagues after a wonderful piece of work in Mumbai when my phone buzzed. I smiled when I saw the message was from Jenny. It read, 'Trevor, we need to talk.' I arranged a telephone call with her for the next morning, intrigued about what she had to say. Jenny was upbeat and energetic during the call. She explained that things had not panned out as they had hoped with Alastair at the helm, and the analysts had been extremely concerned about market sentiment at their annual feedback meeting. Emma and Jenny had decided to return to the business in their old roles and to include Alastair in their executive committee. He had at first been resistant but they had been able to convince him of his importance to the business and he had agreed to stay on. Jenny wanted myself and my partner to assist them over the next year in, as she put it, 'unscrambling the egg'.

Sometimes the parents just can't leave home.

4. Johannesburg

Driving into the large carpark that morning had suddenly triggered a whole series of distant memories for me. I (Trevor) was transported back to my childhood and an exciting trip to the new homeware superstore with my mother and the opportunity to ride in the shiny steel trolley. I remembered a catchy tune from the advert that came on the black-and-white television at 6.15 p.m. each evening, after the news broadcast, which we all sang along to. I was suddenly aware of how much a part of our and many other families' lives this organisation had been, and how strange it felt to be sitting outside their head office waiting to work with them. How my ten-year-old self would have beamed and laughed with joy to see inside the organisation's command centre. I could not help myself and took a moment to call my mother. Nostalgia taken care of, I stepped back into my professional self and with trepidation walked inside the building to meet Paul.

The background

I had been introduced to Paul, the newly appointed CFO (chief financial officer) of the national homeware retail organisation, by their human resources director, who had met me through a mutual colleague. Paul had asked me to help him develop his finance leadership team (FLT).

41

He had just been promoted to the role of CFO, having been the head of the finance department for five years. Paul wanted me to assist with both team development and the transition of Vanessa, his previous second in command, into the head of finance role. The FLT consisted of seven people, including Paul. The whole of the finance team (FT) numbered fifty.

The organisation had until relatively recently been founder-led and run, having been established in 1967. The company had been extremely successful in the homeware retail sector for many years and had become a national household name. Owing to societal, demographic, and cultural changes, the organisation had faced a tough time financially over the last few years. The founder had decided to hand over the reins to a new CEO and chief operating officer (COO), whom he had personally groomed over the years, and the organisation was in the middle of a massive transition process.

They had just spent a huge amount of money on a cultural change intervention by another external consultancy. The purpose of this intervention was described to me as an attempt to create a more inclusive culture that was better at responding to the changes that were taking place in the country. The assessment by this consultancy had identified a need to move from a 'founder-led' culture to a more broad-based leadership culture. They felt that the organisation had not developmentally kept up with their client base. Their recommendation had been that authority and responsibility be more devolved, and that their leadership needed to represent more diversity, which would mirror the client base. The CEO and the COO had therefore expanded the executive team (ET) to ten people.

The reluctant CFO

Paul is a successful, bright, driven, and compassionate person. He is spoken about as a bit of a genius who graduated top of his postgraduate class. He is also known for caring deeply for his staff, though by his own admission he can let them get away with too much. He has a reputation for being pragmatic and getting the job done, something which takes its toll when he has to cover for sub-par performances in the team. Vanessa is known in the organisation as being pragmatic and hard-working, and someone who gets the job done. As a pair, they function incredibly well and carry the finance department. Where Paul is easy on others, Vanessa holds people to account. She can, in her own words, be a hard taskmaster.

Promoting Vanessa was an easy choice for Paul. They had worked together for many years; in fact they had studied together at university and done their articles together. Vanessa had been the one who had encouraged him to join the organisation. They were a formidable team who trusted each other implicitly and, according to Paul, they 'finished one another's sentences'. Paul felt comfortable with Vanessa taking over from him but wanted to ensure that the rest of the FLT were on the same page. However, he was afraid that he would be accused of nepotism.

When I was pitching for the work, both Paul and Vanessa were in the meeting. Together, they provided a rounded picture of both the leadership team and the wider FT. When I enquired what problem they were attempting to solve by bringing me in, they were clear that it was to help to build the FLT into a cohesive and high-performing team. Paul stated that the FT as a whole was functioning well but they were nowhere near where they should be. He believed that he and Vanessa were carrying most of the load. After I had agreed to put together a more detailed proposal for them, they offered to take me on a walkthrough of the department.

What stood out was the layout of the finance department. The team sat in an open-plan configuration, whilst Paul and Vanessa sat in glass-walled offices. When I enquired about this configuration, they explained that they needed quiet in order to get the work done, and didn't feel that it got in the way. I was struck by how defensive they were at the question. I also asked Paul why he still sat with the FT and had not moved upstairs with the rest of the ET. Paul replied that there wasn't really enough space upstairs, but also, in reality, he didn't want to move as his primary relationships were in the FT. He further elaborated that he did not yet really feel part of the ET and would miss his colleagues downstairs. What struck me was twofold. First, Paul was unable or unwilling to leave the FT and take up his executive position. Second, how he and Vanessa's powerful pairing was reinforced by the office layout.

My concern with their pairing was that it disempowered the finance leadership team, both by frustrating the team and letting them off the hook. Vanessa and Paul took on the roles of good and bad parents and allowed the team to remain in a 'childlike' position, meaning they were not being held to account as 'adults'. This would help explain why Paul felt the team was not 'shooting the lights out', and why both he and Vanessa felt they were carrying most of the load.

I pondered Paul's reluctance to move and to take up the executive role enthusiastically. Was the problem as much about Paul's reluctance to leave as it was about what was happening within the ET? Paul had a hero-like status in the FT and I imagined it must be really difficult to give this up. I also wondered if the team, including Vanessa, were as unready to let go of Paul as he was to leave.

After a really positive engagement, I left promising to send through a detailed proposal later that week.

The proposal

Putting together the proposal placed me in a dilemma. What was the best point of intervention? What would be in the best interest of the client—rather than merely address what the client had asked for? I felt that working with Paul alone might be the best way to start. This, I believed, would assist him to understand how his own ambivalence was impacting the team. I called him and very carefully raised the option. Paul was really clear that the team needed the work, and though he was grateful for my offer, insisted that I work with the team as the starting point.

I reluctantly proposed that we run two half-day 'team-building' processes with the FLT, the purpose being threefold: the first being a group diagnostic exercise, to understand what was going on in the team; the second being to pilot OD consulting with the FLT to assess their appetite for ongoing work; the third being to start to prepare the FLT for functioning more independently and becoming, in Paul's words, a high-performance team.

Paul really liked this proposal, and I agreed to put it in writing and get it through to them. Interestingly, Paul said that I needn't do this as he was happy with my verbal description. We agreed on a date and Paul said that he would send out an agenda.

The first team-building session

The first team-building session started off with a storytelling exercise, with each person being asked to share a little information about themselves to help break the ice. This was followed by asking the team to reflect on what each of them expected from the process and what they hoped to achieve. Paul jumped straight in and bolstered up the team by letting them know how important they were to the organisation and how he hoped they would all be open and honest with each other. Yet it was really difficult for the team to get going, and both Paul and Vanessa jumped in often to push the conversation along. Their pairing dominated most of the morning's proceedings. It became clear that the team were suspicious about what the real purpose of the team-building session was and found it difficult to articulate what they wanted to get out of it.

What did reveal itself was that everyone was very clear about what tasks were required of them as members of the FT as well as people managers. They proudly told stories of how task-oriented they were, and how they kept the lights on no matter what. I found it interesting how quickly the conversation jumped to their work tasks, rather than staying with the task of saying something more personal about themselves. The team felt that they produced high-quality work. However, both Paul and Vanessa had privately shared with me their concern that the performance bar of the team was not set very high.

The second exercise of the day was to reflect on the leadership roles of individual members of the team, what leadership meant to them and what was required for this team and for the wider FT.

The team really struggled with this task, and Paul jumped in a few times to praise them in what they did. In fact, over the course of the next few hours, a number of the team asked if they couldn't just be left alone to do their jobs (tasks), or be task managers. The group struggled to articulate how they were currently doing in their leadership roles, what leadership was required of them or this might mean in the FT. When I challenged the group, Paul and

Vanessa jumped in to answer for everyone. Paul again took a strong stand in defining what he thought the roles should be, and again was optimistic that the team had the ability to fulfil these. Vanessa looked more sceptical, at times apprehensively glancing at me, but she didn't contradict Paul.

What this session did bring up was a lot of emotion. The subject of trust, or rather the lack of it, was brought into the room for the first time. The eldest member of the team, Jane, who had been in the company for thirty years, brought it up first and clearly had very strong feelings about what was going on. She said that things had changed too much of late, and that old people like her were no longer needed or trusted.

A few members, including Paul and Vanessa, moved quickly to contain her feelings, which became the focus of the rest of the session. When I reflected that whilst these feelings were important, they were taking us away from the primary task of the session, I was met with strong resistance. I was being shown clearly what was OK and not OK to talk about, and what happened if you went against this. The team needed to offload a lot of emotion on a personal level and it felt that half a day was not enough; in fact, not even three days would be enough.

The group struggled to close the session at the allotted time, but with the promise of the follow-up session two weeks later they reluctantly separated.

The debrief (part 1)

I held a debriefing session with both Paul and Vanessa two days later. They were happy with the overall trajectory of the work but were concerned with the level of unhappiness and lack of 'equal' engagement and accountability of individual members. When I reflected on the power of their pairing and its possible implications for the group, I was answered with a long justification based on how working together for so long obviously meant that they would be a strong pair. They strongly rejected the idea that this might influence the group dynamics.

They were happy to talk more about Jane, who had been so emotional. They reflected on how she wasn't keeping up with technology and resisted change. She had apparently run into trouble a few times with HR for quite aggressive verbal outbursts with newer staff members.

When I enquired about why nothing had been done about this, I was told, 'You know, that's just Jane and she really does her job well.'

I decided to push Paul a bit harder on setting boundaries and giving more direct feedback to Jane. He looked around and then said that he didn't want to escalate things in the team that might impact productivity. Vanessa disagreed openly with Paul, saying that this attitude set a bad example for the rest of the team, and had become somewhat of a norm amongst them. This led to a really productive conversation, with Paul speaking about how he felt that the culture within the ET was strongly critical, and how he felt that because of this he needed to protect his people in finance. He also said that the critical nature of the CEO and COO towards the rest of the ET kept him attached to the FT, even though he knew intellectually that the ET should be his peer group.

The team and in fact the entire department relied heavily on Paul to play the 'heroic' leader. The very thought of him moving on created anxiety for the team, for Vanessa, and for Paul himself. The team had co-created the fantasy of being immobilised without Paul and his pairing with Vanessa. The impact of this on the FLT was that they did not take up leadership roles and merely functioned as task managers.

We finished the debrief by planning for the next half-day team-building session. We agreed, after some negotiation, that we would spend the first part of the session getting feedback on the last session and what had happened in the time between the sessions. The second part of the session would focus on the eventuality of Paul's leaving the team to take up his ET role.

The second team-building session

The session started tentatively with Paul again having to take the lead. Paul then shared his vision of what the team would look like after he moved on. In reality, this had been explained by power-point presentations many times before. However, this was the first time the topic had been the subject of a discussion. Paul again spoke of his confidence in Vanessa to lead the team on her own and of the rest of the FLT to provide the leadership the FT needed.

There were a lot of strong emotions expressed regarding Paul leaving. The team began an attempted negotiation for Paul to stay on longer. Vanessa tried to explain how important it was for the team to form their own identity without Paul, even though this would be difficult. Much anger was directed at her for this suggestion, with one or two people questioning why they had not been considered for the Head of Finance role themselves. Paul jumped to Vanessa's defence, stating she was the most experienced team member and, including himself, one of only three qualified accountants in the team.

Rita, the only other accountant in the group, then spoke up about a rumour doing the rounds in the organisation. She said that people were talking about Paul and Vanessa being involved in a romantic affair. This quite understandably led to much defending and explaining. I tried to reflect that though this discussion was important, it was stopping the group from facing up to the imminent loss of Paul and his pairing with Vanessa. This was met with strong resistance from the group, who wanted to get to the bottom of this slight on Paul's integrity. The rest of the session was spent with the group taking care of Paul's feelings by reassuring him about how he was respected and admired in the organisation.

The group again struggled to end the session, instead wanting to extend it by another two hours. I suggested that we rather put aside some time every two weeks for the team going forwards to continue the discussions we had been having. They, quite surprisingly, agreed to this suggestion. I had thought they would attempt to push me out for attempting to divert the conversation back to the imminent change.

I held a debriefing with Paul and Vanessa the next day.

The debrief (part 2)

Paul and Vanessa were visibly shaken by the group bringing up the rumour. Paul was more concerned for himself and his career; Vanessa's concerns too were more for Paul. They needed a lot of reassurance that I did not believe the rumour, and that I believed such rumours are not unusual about strong pairings like theirs. I enquired whether they had ever had anyone else comment on their closeness over the years and both strongly denied this. They were able to acknowledge that perhaps there was some jealousy of their close relationship.

I reflected that possibly the session was pushed in the direction it went by the group exactly because they wanted Paul to stay and that by revealing the rumour, the team was able to join together in protecting Paul and show their adoration for him. Furthermore, I wondered if bringing up the rumour might not be a form of power play by Rita, the only other person in contention for Head of Finance, and that it was intended to discredit Vanessa. This led to a very productive conversation about how Rita often behaved passive-aggressively towards Vanessa, while she was 'gushing' towards Paul. However, the majority of the debrief session was spent containing both of their anxieties.

Paul ended the debrief by saying he had hoped everything would have been worked through after the second session and that he felt disappointed. I asked if he was able to see the complex dynamics at play for him, Vanessa, and within the wider organisation. He said he was but that he had nevertheless hoped for a quick fix. I was left wondering if Paul really wanted things to change or whether, unconsciously, he really wanted things to stay as they were.

We agreed to allow a few days to pass in order to process what had happened and to meet again the following week to plan the next team session.

Consultant's reflections

Over the next few days I was left pondering what had transpired in this consultation so far. I had a strange feeling of discomfort that just would not go away. When I tried to work out what it might be about, I kept bashing up against the idea that I had been working in the wrong place. Even though I felt that the facilitation itself had gone well, I did not believe that much would actually change.

It was clear that Paul was reluctant to leave his position in the finance team, and that even though he believed in Vanessa, he was not ready to hand over the reins to her properly. He knew objectively what he needed to do, but somehow was unable to follow through with it. Even though I knew that a certain amount of narcissism is essential for an individual to navigate the corporate leadership role, Paul did not come across as excessively narcissistic to me. Yes, he enjoyed being adored and needed by his team—but it did not feel to me that this was what left him reluctant to leave, and over the years of my consulting, my gut feeling has served me well.

Something about the very close relationship between Paul and Vanessa was linked to what was happening in the team—and I didn't mean in the way some of the team interpreted it, i.e. that they were having an affair. I think it was in some way a representation of the entire organisational system, but I couldn't quite work out what. I felt I should have been firmer with Paul about doing some work with him first, before agreeing to the 'team build'.

This is what brought me to the supervision. I felt quite stuck about where to go next. I was aware that working on my own meant I didn't have someone to process with me and point out how I was getting caught up in the group's dynamics.

Supervision conversation

Ajit: What I find really interesting is that on the surface you were brought in to develop the finance leadership team. However, I am left wondering what you were really brought in to do. What was really happening below the surface?

Trevor: Paul was clear that he wanted to prepare Vanessa to be the new head of the team and that the FLT needed to perform better. He felt that I could assist with this, so he asked me to help facilitate with his transition.

Ajit: However, throughout your story, you indicate that he never wanted to move on and take up his role in the executive team, so installing Vanessa is still just 'in theory'. You have seen through both processes and your work with the two of them that he is still firmly in charge. Could it be that he was using you as a smoke screen? He doesn't seem to want to move away, so having you 'develop' the team is his excuse to stay on through the process.

Trevor: That makes me think. If I was there to help the team to transition and develop, I should have focused on the transition element. What I mean is that I perhaps should have pushed the team harder to grieve his moving on in order to help them reconfigure and develop under Vanessa's leadership.

Ajit: Yes, and instead what has happened is that you have ended up working with 'developing' the team whilst Paul is still at the helm—and in effect reinforced his leadership of the team.

Trevor: As I said to you, I had the desire to first process his ambivalence with moving on into the ET. I knew that he found it very difficult to let go and also to pass on the baton.

Ajit: This probably served a purpose for him. You say that he found it very difficult to move and join the executive team that he was a part of. Instead, he fled from this and remained where he felt less anxious. I wonder whether this process enabled him to do this rather than make the transition.

Trevor: That makes sense to me. Why would he want to move on when there was no real benefit, other than the title? He has no authority at the executive level, whereas in the FT he is able to take up his authority and have control. He is respected and admired in his team. Paul said that the ET exists in name alone. That the 'actual' leadership team consists of the CEO and the COO—that are where authority and decision-making lie. He felt impotent there and has little desire to give up his position in the FLT.

Ajit: Can you see now that there seems to be a parallel process emerging? The CEO–COO relationship seems to be parallel to that of Paul and Vanessa.

Trevor: That is really interesting because what I constantly heard was that the CEO–COO had set up an as-if 'executive team' but were in fact always the ones who made the decisions. And what you're pointing out is that Paul and Vanessa are doing the same thing here. I hadn't considered that this was in fact a parallel process.

Ajit: Yes, the underlying 'founder-led' culture seems to continue no matter what change the other consultancy has tried to effect. The leaders of the business perpetuate what has 'always been' under the surface whilst paying lip service to cultural change. It's not just the leaders of the business that perpetuate this; the rest of the organisation also have no real desire for things to change.

Trevor, I wonder whether your 'stuckedness' comes from the fact that on the surface you have been brought in to help develop the team and establish Vanessa's leadership. However, unconsciously, there is little desire for this. Paul does not want to move and is holding on to his position in this team. I wonder whether your work is more to support Paul take up his authority and move into the exec role and help the team mourn his moving on. Because if he does not move on, the team will be stuck—and this is the 'stuckedness' that you are experiencing.

Trevor: That really does resonate. I feel that the whole organisation is in some ways stuck. Stuck in an old operating model, stuck in an old leadership model, and stuck in a time gone by. I'm thinking that the only way for me to get unstuck is to create a space for the team to mourn the loss of Paul and to accept what the new FLT will be. It will be interesting to see how Paul responds to this. However, I have on my side his contacting me to help with the transition. That's how I can remain on task myself without being distracted by the other organisational dynamics.

What next?

I just couldn't get that seventies advert jingle out of my head as I drove to meet Paul. I wondered if it was colonising my thoughts so I didn't have to deal with the anxiety of the upcoming meeting. Whatever the reason for its presence, I knew what had to be done, and it was for that reason that I had arranged this morning's meeting with Paul alone.

Paul was at first slightly guarded and asked again if Vanessa should not be in the meeting. However, he settled into the conversation when I said that I had been taken by surprise when the nature of their relationship was questioned by some of the group. I reassured him that I did not for a moment believe that there was anything untoward in their relationship, and this seemed to relax him even more. I did, however, enquire whether he had noticed any other close relationships in the organisation, and what this might mean. He paused for a bit, then smiled and spoke about the CEO and CFO's relationship, and shared how frustrating he found this and how it got in the way of the ET's ability to function. We spent quite some time exploring why close relationships or pairings were so important in the organisation and he spoke at length of how psychologically unsafe it felt without a close ally or partner.

This conversation allowed us to then discuss his role in the ET. I reflected that I had two roles to undertake in working with him: first, to assist him in moving on from the FLT in order to allow for its development under Vanessa; and second, to help him take up his role on the ET. He spoke for a long while about the dysfunction of the ET and how he had no real authority or influence there. He became quite emotional when I suggested that this was one of the reasons why leaving the FLT must be really difficult. When I asked him why he didn't just decline the CFO role and remain as head of the finance team, he looked shocked, but something had hit home. The ensuing discussion revealed that he was aware he couldn't stay in his current role and had in fact thought it might be best to leave the organisation. It is so interesting that once something is said, it can't be unsaid and, also, how it frees up other conversations. Paul and I agreed that leaving now would be premature and that he really did need to give the CFO role his full commitment. We also agreed that we should continue to meet to coach him through the transition.

He consented to start the next session with the FLT by confirming that he was formally stepping away and that Vanessa would be taking the lead on her own going forward. This was a major step for Paul, and he knew it: letting go and moving on would not be easy. However, he also acknowledged that his presence was holding Vanessa back and he really did have full confidence in her. With that concluded, Paul gave Vanessa a call and it was agreed that the three of us would go out for brunch to discuss the next session.

5. Rio de Janeiro

I (Ajit) have known and worked with ResCo, a Brazilian market research company, for a number of years and have assisted them with a variety of different interventions. I had previously helped one of the directors, Kim, to build her senior leadership team. The intervention, which ran over a number of days, was a success and Kim was really happy with the outcome; on our follow-up, she said that the team was working very well together. A few years later, in the wake of a number of organisational changes, Kim approached me again to conduct a similar intervention.

The organisational context

ResCo conducts privately commissioned market research for international clients who are looking to enter the Brazilian market. The team whom I was asked to assist, division X, gathers information from various sources to assess the market and then advise clients on their business strategy. Their detailed analysis of the market is designed to inform the client organisation's decision-making and strategic priorities for the year ahead.

Division X was made up of about 150 people. Their senior leadership team (SLT) had six members and their direct reports comprised twenty-five team leaders. The division was relatively new, formed under Kim as a part of a strategic shift in the organisation's ways of working. It meant a completely new way of operating for the whole organisation, as every other division now had to use the intelligence that Kim's division produced. This approach brought with it many problems, including conflict and resistance from those other parts of the organisation that were forced to adopt new ways of working. Kim reported that this put a lot of pressure on members of her team; they had to 'constantly keep justifying their existence and ensure they did not make any mistakes in the intelligence they were providing'.

A new CEO had been appointed about a year after Kim set up division X. Kim said that the new CEO was extremely positive about the work of the new division and she finally felt validated and recognised for the hard work the division had put in. Now that the organisation had finally seen its value, she was keen to sort out the dynamics in her leadership teams.

The initial ask

Kim wanted me to replicate some of the work we had done with her previous leadership team. She wanted to create a space where the new team could bond and agree to working principles. She loved the immersive methodology that we had used previously and wanted me to explore similar options.

Her high-level initial diagnosis was that her senior team were very stretched, and that they were unable to delegate to the team leaders below them. It was her observation that they took on too much and did not hold their direct reports to account. This, she felt, was detrimental to both groups. They were unable to get through the volume of work and their direct reports were shirking their responsibility. Together we determined the scope of the work as follows:

A. Develop the SLT; help with building relationships; understand how they were functioning as a team and address any issues that existed.
B. Develop the leadership of the division. This would include the SLT and their direct reports. We would work with them to identify the culture they wanted to create and help them embed this in the division.

One of Kim's clear requirements was that an immersive experience was to be the vehicle of process and dialogue.

Working with another consultancy

We decided to utilise an external consultancy that delivers creative immersive experiences for teams. They use methodology from the performing arts in facilitating change. I was introduced to this consultancy by someone whom I respect and hold in high regard. She spoke highly of their credentials in immersive work.

From the very start of the engagement, I felt a tension between our two approaches. However, I decided to go ahead as I believed that if we approached this with generosity of spirit, the right answer would emerge from the process. The consultancy were dogmatic about their methodology and insistent on creating an activity-based event. I kept pushing back that there was not enough time to process what was going on and that dialogue was a key currency in our work.

At one point, the director of the other consultancy said to me, 'I wouldn't want to keep too much time for process as we don't want to lose energy with people waffling on.' As a consequence, I felt attacked. I also felt that the primary client relationship was mine and I began to feel nervous that the other consultancy were not appreciative of this. I took up my authority and made it very clear that the event or activity was only a vehicle for the process, and if we needed the time to engage in dialogue, then that is what we would do.

The senior leadership team event

The event was held at a museum in São Paulo. As I wandered down the street from my hotel, I was struck by the sheer energy of the city. I felt nervous about the working relationship with the other consultancy but I took inspiration from the city's Latin motto, which I had read the previous day: *Non ducor, duco*, which means 'I am not led, I lead'. I decided I had to take up my authority as I entered this workshop.

We started by getting participants to tell personal stories in order to build a shared narrative. The participants were eager and enthusiastic and, as a team, were engaged and shared some really deep stories with each other. This changed the mood of the room significantly. We then got the group to engage in an exercise using chairs, to constellate the experience of being in the current team. This exercise revealed the strengths of specific relationships and where other relationships needed working on. The exercises were well received, and the group participated energetically. Finally, we got them to give each other feedback on how they were working both individually and as a team. Each member took turns to sit in the hot seat while everyone else gave them feedback on their experience of them. This was a powerful process which I had to facilitate and hold very carefully but which proved to be very impactful.

We debriefed the process and distilled the key points that they would take back to the office. This was a difficult process for me as I felt I was in conflict with the other consultancy, who wanted to get on with the agenda of more activities. However, I stood my ground and we took the process to a deeper level, which was very useful for the group. Following this, the group agreed that they wanted to create a similar exercise for their next level of leadership and were keen to bring them into the process. Afterwards, Kim was very excited. She commented on the success of the event and was eager to start preparing for the larger group workshop.

Follow-up

The next day I was invited to an SLT meeting back in the office to design the new event. I invited the other consultancy to join this meeting. However, they were unable to do so as they had other commitments whilst out in Brazil. I was irritated by this but decided to continue anyway.

The SLT was energised by the planning process, yet I was struck by two things. The first was the level of detail they went into and the second was the level of anxiety I felt in the room. Whilst mostly the same design as before, this next process would involve many more people, so we collectively decided to utilise a dialogue-based social network technology platform to cater for the large-group format. It was also decided that the larger group would be given an opportunity to ask the leadership team questions about the future direction of their division. The leadership team was very anxious about this particular exercise and I was left wondering what they might be afraid of hearing. They constantly questioned the value of it but finally deferred to Kim to make a decision about it. We eventually agreed that part of the purpose of the next workshop would be to give the larger group a chance to reflect on the current culture within the division and what a high-performance culture might look like.

We further agreed to use the performing arts consultancy we had previously used to assist us again.

In my meeting with the other consultancy, I made it known that I was disappointed they had not attended the client meeting. I felt like I had to remind them of my authority and relationship with the client. We agreed that we needed to have a conversation about how we would work together before we embarked on the second workshop. We agreed that the idea of process would take precedence and whilst there would be a running order and a schedule of activities, we would take stock as the day went by and be prepared to change direction if that's what the group needed. We also agreed that I would use my judgement to decide this and that the consultant team would follow my lead.

The management team workshop

The workshop was scheduled to take place in Rio de Janeiro and the team was to fly in from all over Brazil for this session. I arrived a few days in advance to check the arrangements and ensure the other consultancy was prepared and on task. We met the night before and ran through the schedules, and I went to bed feeling prepared for the day ahead.

The workshop ran according to the agenda, but a number of curious things happened. First, the other consultancy arrived at the venue almost forty-five minutes earlier than the agreed time. They had set up and were waiting when I got there. The set-up was not as agreed, so I had to reorganise the space for the first session. I could sense their irritation at me for rearranging the room. However, in my mind, this was what we had agreed to at the prep meeting the previous night.

Second, right at the start of the day, Kim came to tell us that two out of six of her senior leadership team were not going to be present. She said that although she was disappointed, the day should continue as planned. As the day proceeded, other members of the larger group started leaving, with a varied number of excuses. Kim was angry as she felt she had paid a lot of money for this event and had blocked it in her team's diaries well in advance.

The conversation at the end of the day was a revealing one in which the wider group spoke of the difficulties of working in the division. They described being unable to assert their own authority. The group also said that they were constantly waiting to 'get their homework marked' by the SLT, which meant that every time they finished a piece of work, they expected it to have multiple revisions from those above them. This led to a defensive conversation between the two levels of leadership, each pointing fingers at the other with regards to what was getting in the way of 'high performance'.

With respect to the other consulting team, I found that they continually took a backseat, providing no support in co-facilitating the process with the large group. Occasionally, they even sat outside the group and engaged in their own conversations. At the end of the first day, I brought this up with them and said that I didn't feel like we had worked together as a team. It felt like two consultancies doing their own thing and it seemed fragmented. They suggested that there was too much process and too little action—and this was the only reason for the event not playing out as we had hoped.

The next day, before we started, Kim took me aside to say she was very upset as overnight two other members of her leadership team had contacted her to say that they could not make it to the workshop. She said that of the six, we would now only be joined by two. I listened to her and acknowledged that she was possibly feeling abandoned by her leadership team. I asked her what she wanted to do, and she said that she would like us to proceed as planned. I reflected on how I was also feeling abandoned by the consultant team and how difficult I was finding the whole process.

At the final check-out process, the group reported how valuable they had found the interaction and that they were energised to take this back to their teams. Kim came up to me and said that whilst she was disappointed in her leadership team, she was very happy that the others had seemingly embraced the process and was excited to see what they would take back to their teams.

At the final debrief with the other consultancy group, they said they were delighted with the feedback. I was so tired at the end of the last few days that I didn't feel like getting into a full debrief conversation with them at this point. However, in my mind, I had already decided that I would not be working with them again. I felt very let down by them, especially as they had come so highly recommended to me by my colleague and mentor. Exhausted, I left Rio.

A few weeks later, one of my colleagues collated all the notes on the flip charts and sent this information through to Kim to share with her team. We immediately got a response back that the flip-chart notes were not 'up to the mark'. I called Kim to speak with her and she said that her leadership team had said that they were very disappointed in the notes. They said that the information wasn't helpful as it didn't give them any fresh insights or suggest a way forward, and that this was a direct reflection of the day. When I probed into what had happened since the workshops, she said that nothing had happened as the group was waiting for the notes to guide them, and, because they were so weak, they could not continue. I agreed to have a video conference with her to process what had happened with the notes.

Consultant's reflections

This was a difficult engagement for me. I had an existing relationship with Kim and I was keen to help her out and do a good job for her. I believed I had taken a risk in partnering with the other consultancy. I felt it was remiss of me not to have engaged in a detailed contracting process with them. What I mean by this is not a legal contracting process but an in-depth dialogue on philosophy and methodology. Instead, as speed was of the essence, I had decided to move fast.

I was unable to make sense of their extreme opposition to working in a partnering way. It felt very much like they wanted to do their thing while I did mine. Even though they were trained in co-facilitation, they did not even attempt to support me. And if I intervened during their allocated time slots, it was a difficult interaction. It felt like there was a strong competitive element to the relationship. However, as I had brought them in, I could not see why I would feel competitive. I had wanted to do the best job for Kim.

Also, I was curious as to what degree the consulting team mirrored the dynamics of the client system. I was left wondering to what extent me feeling abandoned was a reflection of what was going on for Kim and how I could have used this data in the moment—both with my team and also to make an effective intervention. I think I was so caught up in the dynamic that I found it difficult to step aside. Lastly, in retelling this story, what struck me was that I also had another consultant from my own business supporting the event. However, I seemed to have completely erased them from the story and focused entirely on my individual tussle with the other consultancy. I wondered what that was about.

So, my supervision question was: what did I miss and what did I get caught up in?

Supervision conversation

Trevor: There are two things to consider here. One is the relationship with the other consultancy and the second is what happened in the client system. Let's deal with this as two separate parts that we can integrate after we interrogate each one. One is about the client system and the other is about your consulting system. There may or may not have been an overlap. Which one do you want to unpack first?

Ajit: Let's go to the client system first. I am curious as to why that failed and why we ended up where we did.

Trevor: It seems to me that the first process with the senior leadership team worked really well. Feedback was good, there was a positive experience, and it seems like you created safety. Therefore, the team could come together in a cohesive manner. The question I am left with is: what was the purpose of the second workshop?

Ajit: The idea was to take what we had created and build it into the layer below.

Trevor: If I am hearing you correctly, you wanted to create the same sense of cohesion and build the team. So, help me understand why you changed the process?

Ajit: I didn't really change the process. What we did was something that would work with a larger group of people, rather than the intimate workshop with the smaller group.

Trevor: I get that, but what I am talking about is why you put in the piece about feedback, where there was a space to give feedback to the superiors. You describe in detail the second planning meeting and how much anxiety was in the room and how detail-oriented it was. Why do you think they were so anxious?

Ajit: To me, it was the anxiety of exposure to the wider team. And you are making me consider that the detail-orientation was really about this anxiety. There was something strong in the system about hierarchy and how they would come across to the next level. I guess I didn't see this in the first session, as Kim wanted to create a different environment with her team that was free from those hierarchical dynamics. And perhaps I missed this during the planning meeting.

Trevor: There seems to have been a lot of anger in this process. And you experienced this as anger towards the other consultancy. Could this have distracted you from noticing the anger in the client system from the leadership team to Kim? It finally reveals itself when they don't show up for the rest of the workshops. It feels like they felt shamed and angry that Kim had put them in a position where they had to receive feedback from their teams in an open forum. They then reject her workshop design by not showing up—which means they can't get the feedback. When you send through the notes, that's an easy target, as they cannot openly attack Kim and so, instead, they attack you and the notes.

Ajit: So, then, what do you make of what happened in the consultant team? It feels almost like we were a mirror of the client system. Or were we?

Trevor: The senior leadership team rejected the design and the other consultancy seems to have rejected the design—you turned up the next morning and they had redesigned the workshop without telling you. They also resisted working with your model and engaging in the dialogue. In the first piece, you took control; but there was something in the design of the second piece that everyone seems to have been uncomfortable about. The design was perhaps the absolute correct thing to do, but in not attending to the discomfort, I am left wondering what has been missed.

Ajit: If I hear you correctly, what you are suggesting is that perhaps my next move needs to be to work with Kim and her SLT to help them voice what the discomfort was about. This may unlock something in their relationship. It will also give Kim the ability to talk about how she felt when they didn't show up on the final days. This is perhaps diagnostic of how they work together in their day-to-day as well. And a forensic and honest evaluation of this process may unlock something about their ways of working and what is being defended against. Anything you would suggest about the other consultancy?

Trevor: It feels almost like they were mirroring with you how the SLT was behaving with Kim. And if you plan to work with them again, an honest evaluation of this piece of work is imperative. It will be difficult for you to stay curious, as you have been caught up in a dynamic process. That's why I say, if you intend on working with them again, reparation is required. If not, why bother?

What next?

Four weeks after the event, I contacted Kim to plan a follow-up. She said she was very disappointed with the progress her team made after the workshop. She felt that a lot of headway was achieved on the day, but there was no transfer back to the office. There was a feeling that the participants did not take up their roles and bring anything back. She said that the next level down had no understanding of what had happened. She felt abandoned by her leadership team and did not feel supported. We were able to come to an agreement that the notes had become an object of attack and were being used as a way to defend the team's inability to act.

We explored what happened in the process; in other words, hers was about abandonment but what did she think happened to the others? In what way did this whole intervention impact them? This was a profound question for her to think about as we started opening up how they actually work together on a day-to-day basis and how this dynamic is not new. It only got heightened in the two days as the simulated environment of the workshop played out, which in my experience is often the case. When you take away the usual trappings of work, the dynamic becomes far rawer and more exposed. This line of enquiry helped Kim to start seeing what role she had probably played in this process. We spoke about how she and I paired up to design an intervention and perhaps the others felt left out and unable to contribute to the design due to our overwhelming enthusiasm. They were perhaps anxious and unable to voice their anxiety due to the inherent hierarchical nature of the business.

We agreed on a session with her SLT in order to help them work through what was getting in the way of moving ahead with implementing the takeaways from the larger group session. This was an important next step as the SLT had not had time to come together to make sense of the experience and to work out their role in what had gone on. I said that it would be important to engage in an open conversation about how the SLT and Kim as leaders of this department were crucial in setting the tone and contributing to the culture and behaviours that we were witnessing. She knew that this would be a tough conversation, but she also knew that this was the intervention that the SLT really needed.

6. Nairobi

The experience of growing up as a child in different parts of Africa never leaves your bones and arriving in Nairobi's Jomo Kenyatta International Airport activated those old feelings instantly. Kenya has always held a special place in my (Trevor's) family's hearts. My father had spent much of his time working there while we were growing up and he kept us entertained with stories from this beautiful country. He had befriended Duncan K, a work colleague from Nairobi, early on in his time in Kenya. Duncan and his family became very special to our whole family and I was looking really forward to catching up with him and his wife on this trip.

I had spent much of my early childhood growing up as a white child in apartheid South Africa, where having an African man stay in our house was unusual to say the least, and whenever Duncan came to stay with us many eyebrows were raised in the neighbourhood. Duncan and my father had a wonderfully mischievous ritual that left an indelible mark on me. Duncan had apparently come up with the plan on a flight with my father to South Africa in the early seventies, no doubt after one whiskey too many. He wanted my father to play chauffeur to him on their drive to our house in Durban when they arrived the next morning. Seeing as how they would both be in suits, all they needed was a suitable hat for my father. Apparently they knew the co-pilot quite well and when they shared their plan with him, he gladly loaned them the required head gear. So after collecting their luggage, with my father carrying it all of course, Duncan had the backdoor of the car opened for him and they drove to our house in rush-hour traffic, with Duncan waving to all and sundry. We were having breakfast when these two men rolled into our kitchen in hysterics, telling us of the shocked faces of those in the other cars.

That story and what my father and Duncan taught me about race and difference have stayed with me my whole life. They showed me and my brothers that we should never shy away from confronting inequalities and should always deal with such difficulties with humour and pranks. I could not wait to see Duncan again on this trip to relive his telling of those times.

The company

There are some consulting contracts that really resonate with you and this was one of those. About two years earlier, I had decided to embark on a part-time training programme to qualify as a wildlife and trails guide. I have always been passionate about wildlife and tend to spend much of my free time in wildlife reserves in Africa, so training as a guide had always been at the back of my mind. I had come across an amazing organisation in the Maasai Mara National Reserve that could provide me with both distance learning as well as intensive practical training in the field. The company had a wonderful track record for training guides throughout Africa and had over the last few years also branched out into training people to work in anti-poaching units throughout the continent. Over the past two years, I had completed the theoretical and practical components of the qualification with them, and during my last trip I had undertaken an intensive tracking practical for three weeks.

It was during this trip that the owners of the company, Norman and Felix, had a conversation with me around the fire one night about how I might be able to assist them with their growth and expansion as an organisation. They had been approached by a very well-known documentary company who wanted to film on the numerous wildlife reserves owned or occupied by their company. The content was to be used on one of the popular video-streaming services that broadcast around the world, and would provide global exposure and advertising for the company. The actual filming rights would not be paid for, but the company's vehicles and guides would be involved in the documentary productions, so in reality the opportunity would provide free exposure and advertising to potentially millions of prospective clients. It sounded on paper like a win–win situation. The question we threw around the fire that night was what the possible impact of shifting from their core business might be.

The company had been in business for over twenty-five years and had become the go-to training institution globally for would-be guides. Norman and Felix had met whilst working at an upmarket lodge when they were in their early twenties and had become a formidable team. Norman drew on the knowledge he had gained from studying zoology in the UK, as well as a good English school education, to entertain foreign clients; whilst Felix used his unmatched tracking abilities to ensure that the guests were treated to the most amazing wildlife sightings. Although educated in the UK, Norman had been born in Kenya and had grown up in an entrepreneurial family, who had encouraged him from a young age to be independent and not expect things to be handed to him on a plate. Felix, on the other hand, was born into the local Maasai tribe and grew up in a village very close to the Maasai Mara. He had spent his entire life in the 'bush' and had been taught how to track animals by the elders of his village. The two men developed a strong friendship and profited together from all the foreign currency tips they received. The lodges and safari companies loved them for good reason, and they were in high demand as a team.

Felix told an amazing story about attending to livestock as a teenager and losing all trace of one cow. Maasai people are often viewed as a nomadic tribe who follow their herds to better grazing lands and water. This is not the case. Seasonal cattle herd migration is usually done by the *morani* (young warriors), while the rest of the family and small livestock remain at the main homestead. Fearing that the cow might fall prey to the local lion pride and that he would have to return home with fewer cattle than he'd left with, Felix and the other *morani* were able to locate that one cow whilst closely monitoring the predators, including lions and hyenas, which were in the vicinity. Such were the tracking abilities of the Maasai people.

It was not too long before safari lodges and companies recruited the two of them to train young potential guides and trackers from all over Kenya. They did this successfully for a few years, until they spotted an opportunity to set up their own operation training guides and trackers, and thereby provide a steady stream of graduates for the industry. They started small and offered eighteen-month training programmes for prospective students. The industry loved them and soon they were training graduates for placements throughout Africa. They were even asked to train staff for certain National Parks Organisations across Africa. They started by providing the training only in Kenya but soon had set up training institutions in a few other Southern African countries as well.

Poaching has always been a problem in Africa and over the last decade the rhino had become the new target species. Rhino horn, quite incorrectly, had become highly sought after for traditional potions in certain parts of the world. The rhino population was diminishing quickly and anti-poaching units were required throughout Africa. Felix and Norman saw the opportunity to add this training to their repertoire and had recruited an expert in the field from South Africa to set up and manage this new endeavour.

News of their training spread internationally and they started getting students from all over the world, who came to spend a year learning the trade of guiding and tracking. As I had discovered to my own benefit, they had moved with the times and had begun to provide an online learning component to their training, which allowed working people like myself to conduct the theoretical part of their course virtually and then to do intensive practical placements in different game reserves around Africa.

Beginning with our conversation that night, and continuing over the next few weeks of my stay to complete my practical module, the three of us put together a plan for how best to incorporate the documentary company into their business. We worked out who would deliver the content and how they would also be able to offer prospective students the opportunity to experience documentary film making first hand. We agreed that I would come back in four months' time to do a full evaluation of how it was working and to provide an independent perspective for the two of them. What was even better was that we agreed that we would barter my services for a waiver of my tuition fees, which were starting to build up. Hopefully we would both win!

The consultation

Coming in to land on a game reserve runway strip is always loads of fun. First, you have to do a low flyover of the runway to check for any animals who might be lazing around on the strip; you then initiate a 'go around' and circle round a second time to land. This morning, it was just getting warm and a family of warthog were enjoying the early pickings. The sound of the Cessna chased them off, tails in the air, and we were finally able to touch down.

It was wonderful to be back in the bush and I was pleased to see Samson, my instructor, waiting in the open-top Land Rover at the side of the grass strip. 'Jambo, Trevor!' he shouted as I climbed out of the plane and made my way over to him. We drove slowly to the tented camp that would be my home for the next three weeks, while Samson shared stories of what was happening in and around the camp. I was informed that the Mufasa pride—yes, The Lion King was big in Kenya—was around camp constantly and had killed a big buffalo the evening before.

The camp was just how I remembered it, only a little drier and dustier than usual. Grace, the camp mother, greeted me warmly and showed me to my tent. She explained that brunch was to be served in thirty minutes and I should come and meet everyone over the meal. I could then discuss both my tracking training and my consulting programme with the team.

The group at brunch was quite big, with one cohort of ten students who were just about to finish their year of training and a second group of twelve students who were two months into their year. The trainees who had been there for nearly twelve months were mostly older and from Germany and Scandinavian countries. The new candidates were younger than I was used to, and Grace told me that the watoto (children) were all around eighteen years of age and just out of school. I sat with the instructors, whom I knew well, and they introduced me to the two new backups who had arrived from Namibia the week before.

Samson pointed out a small group, including Erik, an instructor I knew well, who were sitting to the one side. He referred to them as the 'Attenborough group' in a manner that was more disparaging than I was used to hearing from him. They were, I gathered, the documentary film crew. I walked over to say hi to Erik and to introduce myself to the rest of the group, but was interested by their slightly standoffish demeanour. I could also not help noticing how everyone else watched me suspiciously as I spoke to the film crew. I could see that Samson was slightly uncomfortable when I returned to the table. He jokingly asked how the Attenborough group were doing. I laughed and made some small talk about Erik's new beard, knowing, however, that this was a conversation that we would need to revisit properly.

Fortunately, at that point Grace called me away to the lecture tent to sort out my paperwork and to collect the new dark green uniform I had ordered. She informed me that I would be doing extensive tracking work with Samson over the next three weeks. I would be expected to undertake weekly practical field observation examinations and in between these Samson and I would be tracking with the *mzungu* (white people) and *watoto* groups. It was the first time that I had experienced groups of people being given names and when I enquired about it Grace laughed a little uncomfortably.

Over the next few days tracking lions was all Samson and I did; we had daily sightings of the Mufasa pride from the Land Rover, and a few close encounters on foot too. We were expected to call in each sighting to camp on the handheld radios we carried in our backpacks, a protocol which I found slightly unusual. What was more unusual for me was that we were asked to stand down from encounters within fifteen minutes so that the film crew could come in and get footage. We needed to withdraw quite far from the sighting as the film crew could not have any people or other vehicles in their shots.

Each time a group was asked to stand down, the grumblings and snide comments about the 'Attenborough' group grew in intensity. What was more interesting to me was that the splitting occurred not just between the students and the film crew, but also between the two groups of students. In effect, there were now four distinct groups in camp:

the *watotos*, the *mzungus*, the Attenboroughs, and the instructors and staff group. There was an uneasy feeling in camp around the fire at night and the anxiety I felt was unusual for me in this environment. The one saving grace for the entire camp was the nearby nightly calls of the lion pride, reminding us to be on our guard as they were known to wander through the camp on occasion. Midnight visits to the toilet were anxiety provoking, to say the least.

The incident

The animals had been louder that night than usual and there had been the distinctive cough of a leopard interspersed with lion and hyena calls. I had lain awake for some time and was jolted out of my sleep by Samson very early the next morning. It was still dark and extremely cold outside the tent, and we had some coffee around the newly made fire with six of the younger students. Samson briefed the group that he was certain the leopard had been hunting in the night and had cached its kill somewhere in the drainage line a few kilometres from camp.

The sun was just coming up when we got out of the drop-off vehicle quite close to the drainage line. The tracks of a large male leopard were distinctive and were accompanied by drag marks, indicating it had killed something during the night. What was disconcerting was that there were fresh lion tracks alongside. Samson and I both walked to the side to load our 375 rifles and then briefed the group on instructions for the walk and how potentially dangerous the situation might be. About twenty minutes later we heard and then saw two lionesses at the base of a large marula tree. They were staring up at the top branches, where a large male leopard had perched itself and the impala female it had caught. We had hit the jackpot, and as we were downwind we had not yet been seen by the lions; their attention remained fixed on the potential meal in the tree.

As the new protocol required, Samson radioed camp and let them know about the sighting. He arranged that we would spend around twenty minutes with the animals and then slowly withdraw to allow the second group of students to take our place. After another twenty minutes, the film crew would then come in closer with their vehicle.

That's when things got interesting. About ten minutes after we had radioed into camp, we heard the distinctive sound of the film crew's vehicle. They were coming pretty close to the animals and this diverted the lions' attention away from the leopard in the tree. In that moment, the lions became aware of us and were clearly not too happy to see us. Samson radioed the crew on the designated channel to clarify what they were doing and why the second group of students were not in the vehicle instead, as had been agreed.

Tempers began to fray, with the film crew using colourful language to inform Samson that they had first access to multiple animal encounters and that we should withdraw; they would let us know when we could return. Apparently they had been granted this authorisation by Norman and Felix. Arguing in the middle of an encounter with dangerous animals is never a good idea and rather than escalate the situation, Samson briefed the group that we would attempt to retract ourselves without causing the lions to charge at us. The final instruction to the group as we left was: 'If the lions move towards us, do not run; in the bush, the only thing that runs is food.'

When we got back to camp, things were tense, to say the least. The older student group, the *mzungus*, were irate that they had not been included in the morning walk as they needed encounters with wildlife to complete their certification. The younger students, in return, felt that the older group were being patronising towards them. Both groups grew even angrier as the minutes passed and the film crew had not radioed in to say they were leaving the sighting as agreed. In fact, attempts to get hold of them on the radio failed to get a response.

It was a full hour and a half later that the radio call came through to say that the leopard had clumsily dropped the impala, which was immediately grabbed by the lions and the leopard had then left the tree and run off. The anger in camp was palpable, and it was now being directed at Norman and Felix. The students started to band together against the two owners, questioning whether the groups were of any importance to the company—or was film making now what was most important. This played out that evening around the fire, while the film crew stayed away from the rest of us, remaining around their tents and on their mobile phones.

The explosive group meeting

A few uncomfortable days later, we got a message from Grace that Norman and Felix were coming into camp to have a meeting with everyone. I got a sense that the film crew had had a conversation with them and this was what the meeting was to be about. I had tried to get hold of the two of them to discuss what was happening but could not get through, and I thought that my task—as agreed with them—was to observe what was happening and to give my feedback at the end of the three weeks.

That morning's student activity was cancelled and at 10 a.m., as agreed, everyone gathered around the outdoor dining area. Norman and Felix arrived an hour and a half late to a hot, hungry and irritable gathering of people. Norman, who was normally extremely eloquent and to the point, entered into a rambling monologue about compassion, understanding, and the importance of team work. He told the group of students how privileged they were to be in the environment they were in, and that in the real world of the lodges, they would have to learn to share sightings on a daily basis. It was clear that he was uncomfortable having this conversation and that he had only heard part of the story from the film crew and had not discussed what had happened with the instructors.

The students collectively pushed back strongly, bringing up numerous things the film crew had done over the last few months that transgressed camp rules. Everyone got defensive and it became an 'us versus them', 'he said, she said' disagreement. The students questioned the owners' commitment to their education and training, and accused the owners of selling out to viewer numbers.

Sides were taken and the ability to see the different aspects of a complex situation were lost. The meeting ended with Norman attempting to assert his authority quite forcefully and the student and instructor groups disengaging with him. I chose to remain silent as I didn't believe my role ought to be that of facilitator and, if I did so, thought I would lose credibility on all sides. As a mentor of mine once said: 'If you are invited to a friend's house for dinner, don't try to rearrange the furniture.' Things were uncomfortably quiet over brunch and I decided to give Norman and Felix some time alone before I approached them to talk through what had happened.

The debrief

The three of us sat in the lecture tent later that afternoon in order to try to make sense of what had been happening. I realised that the situation was precarious and that both Norman and Felix were feeling quite brittle, and I did not want to increase their defensiveness. Maintaining my bond with them was essential if I were to stand any chance of helping them to see what was happening.

I asked them what they felt had occurred and how they viewed the whole situation. They were angry that the students and the instructors could not see how valuable the presence of the film crew was to the success of the company. They felt that the students were being selfish in not wanting to share sightings and that this did not bode well for their future employment in the industry. I tentatively enquired what they had received in terms of feedback from the instructors. Unfortunately this set them both off on a rant about how they felt that the instructors had taken sides and turned against them, and influenced the students in that direction too.

I agreed with them that the camp had in fact split into distinct different sides; however, I cautioned that attributing blame to any one side would not help us in understanding what was really going on. This triggered both of them, leading them to question whose side I was on in this whole process. It took some time to contain their anger and to repair the disruption in our relationship. I ended our debrief session by saying that everyone had become very stressed over the last few weeks and that some time out would not hurt anyone.

Fortunately, the film crew was about to end their rotation and a new crew was about to start. We agreed to call all of the instructors and current film crew in and to reinforce the standard operating procedures with regards to game sightings. This was done early the next morning and it felt like a sticking plaster that would hold the anxiety for some time at least. Norman and Felix ended the meeting on a strong note, apologising to the leadership team for not having discussed the situation with them first before speaking to the students. They did this with no prompting from me at all, which left me feeling hopeful.

Norman, Felix and I had a coffee together before they left and they informed me that they would be in London in two weeks' time to speak to a possible investor. They knew I would also be in London then and suggested we meet so that I could share my assessment of my experiences in the camp and for the three of us to brainstorm what steps could be taken next. I left them at the airstrip with a positive feeling about our relationship, but was well aware that the situation needed working through as the container of the standard operating procedures and the new crew would not hold for long.

I sat at the bar in the Nyama restaurant back in Nairobi on my last evening in Kenya waiting for Duncan and his wife to arrive for our planned dinner. I was really excited to see them both after such a long break and wondered if they had kept that mischievous spirit I remembered so well. Duncan did not disappoint. Though much older than I remembered, he strode through the door bellowing *"Jambo zungu!"* wearing an old airline pilot's hat. It was going to be a wonderful evening.

Consultant's reflections

During my last few days in camp I had some time to reflect on my experiences, and was left with three different questions that I tried to make sense of. The first was that when I'd moved between the groups to discuss their experiences of what had happened, I was able to appreciate their points of view. They were very clear on what their reasons were for being in the camp and what they had signed up for. What they could not do was empathise with the other groups or appreciate that their reasons for being in the camp might differ.

The second question I was left with was around whether the different groups were unwittingly being set up against each other in competition for the scarce resource of encounters with dangerous animals. If they were guiding paying clients at a commercial lodge, the process of timings for sightings would be very clearly stipulated and there would be no competition.

Third, I was left I questioning whether the owners and guides (on camera) had been seduced by the fame of being on TV.

What brought me into the supervision conversation were those three questions and my assumption that bringing in a documentary company had caused a rupture in the camp. The people had split into four different groups, each with different goals. I wanted to make sense of what had happened and also help the owners see what they were missing in order to take the company forward.

Supervision conversation

Ajit: What was your primary task? Why were you there?

Trevor: The reason I was there was to train as a ranger. I thought I was making a good deal by taking up their offer to consult to them on their expansion and new proposition. And on reflection, I blurred my roles from being a student to being a consultant. So, I had a dual task.

Ajit: Trevor, I want to remind you of a previous conversation we had about your blurring the boundaries of your role. In that story, it was about being consultant or therapist. Here it is about being a consultant or student. I am only pointing out how this seems to happen to you in groups repeatedly. And therefore where does this leave you when you try to make an intervention? How does the group respond or see you? This was very evident when you spoke of how you crossed the boundaries of the groups on the first day to meet with the film crew. You seem to have become some sort of interlocutor between groups. So, for you, there does not seem to be a natural home in this system. That goes back to my question of why were you there in the first place.

Trevor: That makes sense because I don't then belong to any group. And the interesting part is that even as a student, I am not joining either of the cohorts: I am doing an individualised programme.

Ajit: So your role as a consultant was actually obscured—you were there to gain from the experience. How could you keep your relational distance? How could you maintain your objectivity, as you were caught up in the dynamic of needing to have x number of sightings for yourself?

Trevor: That is interesting because I always got preference over everyone—especially the morning of the incident.

Ajit: That is very important. In this story, what I don't seem to have fully understood is the purpose of this organisation. If the purpose is to provide high-quality ranger education to students, then the organisation seems to be engaging in a number of other activities that are detracting from that purpose. The process of making the deal with you is a parallel process to agreeing to the filming. Both you and film crews get the attention and the status of being more important than the students for which the organisation actually exists. So in effect you are in competition with the students and are in a parallel process to the film crew. If you consider feelings as data, what do you think is now going on in the dynamic in the system—based on your own feelings?

Trevor: What comes up for me is a process of envy. I am thinking that each group becomes more envious of the other. The students become envious of the film crew; the instructors are envious of those who are in the film. Actually it is envy and competition: it is a question of both who's up and who's down, but also who is near and far from the action.

Ajit: OK, but what does this tell you about the organisational system, then?

Trevor: The owners thought they were getting free consulting and advertising to grow their business. What they didn't realise was that it actually cost them by creating a dynamic within the system. It took them away from their primary task of education and instead got them focused on other activities. Whilst these other activities were crucial for growth, it feels like they were in competition with the primary task of education. That is what I am learning about the system.

Ajit: This explains the associations with envy and competition. Also, what is interesting is that if the film crew was there to promote the business, why was it making a documentary focused on the reserve rather than on the teaching techniques and methods?

Trevor: You are right; the documentary seems to have become the point of competition with the students, as the film crew were given the privilege of sightings—for which the students had paid money and which they required for their certification.

Ajit: This may seem a left-field question but are Norman and Felix on the same page? In your view, is there competition at that level?

Trevor: What is unspoken about is the race relations in Kenya and how Norman and Felix embody this difference. The power differential between the two of them—a white, privately educated man and a black tribesman—is huge but at the same time not named. And this unconscious competition perhaps gets into the system.

Ajit: I was struck by why the foreign group was called the *mzungu* group. You say this was the first time this happened. And from my knowledge of Kenya, isn't *mzungu* a disparaging term for white people?

Trevor: Yes, I wonder whether this was the system's way of raising the race relations issue as both Norman and Felix did not oppose it. So I guess my work needs to be at the level of Felix and Norman to begin with.

Ajit: Yes, you need to help them get on the same page. So perhaps you need to consider a conversation with Felix and Norman about the purpose of their business and to bring them back to basics. I wonder then if you could get them to locate themselves in the future to create a picture of what the growth would look like. Then to outline the activities that they need to engage in—all aligned with the purpose that they are trying to achieve. This may help to point out any of the competitive elements in this engagement.

What next?

The weather could have not been more different to the Mara when I stepped out of Holborn tube station on my way to meet Norman and Felix that morning. They were already sitting at a table, sipping their drinks, when I entered the coffee shop. Gone was their usual khaki attire and they looked dapper in dark suits. Their usual greeting of '*Jambo, rafiki yangu*' ('hello, my friend'), however, warmed up the morning more than any coffee could.

We exchanged pleasantries about our various travels and experiences, and they shared with me details of the exciting funding meeting they had the previous evening. That was the perfect 'in' to the real reason for our meeting. I offered up my interpretation that whilst being completely understandable, the bringing in of the film crew had created a split in the organisation and had resulted in there now being numerous primary tasks for different groups in the camp and most likely the company as a whole.

Felix nodded thoughtfully while Norman got visibly agitated. It was the first time that I had seen the two of them split in that way. Norman said that it was the bringing in of the film company that had facilitated the generous offer of investment they had just received. I reflected to him that I was in no way suggesting that bringing in the film crew was an incorrect decision, but rather that the manner in which they had been contracted, and that the alignment of the crew's and the company's primary task had not being clearly defined, were the factors that had created the problem. This fortunately made Norman curious and seemed to calm him down.

I asked the two of them what they really wanted from the company, moving forward. They were both slightly sheepish at first but with a little coaxing admitted that they felt that they were ready to cash in on some of their investment and wanted to sell off a portion of the company. I reassured them that I completely understood this and supported them wholeheartedly. I asked what they were actually selling and what vision they had for the company, going forward: was it to continue to be an educational and training entity or were they selling a wildlife/safari company? They were both very clear that what they had built and what they were selling was a wildlife guide and custodial training institution.

This opened up a conversation about whether this ought to be what the film crew were documenting, and whether their role as owners ought to be to clarify and reinforce this as the crew's primary task. Norman was slightly concerned that the crew might just leave if more boundaries were imposed on them; however, Felix stepped in and confidently assured him that there were many documentary companies who would love to have access to their success story. Norman then became excited and the two of them went off on a tangent about how amazing it would be if a documentary resembling the reality shows *Survivor* or *The Amazing Race* were to take off globally. It took some quick thinking to remind them that they were experts at wildlife guide training and not running a TV production company. They both saw what was happening and roared with laughter, and we were glared at by the rest of the people in the coffee shop. Norman quipped, 'Us Africans will never fit in in London,' and Felix quickly responded, 'My friend, you so quickly forget that you are a *mzungu!*'

7. Paris

It was an ordinary winter's morning in London. Wrapped up against the cold wind, I (Ajit) made my way through the labyrinth of lanes near Liverpool Street. It was time for a coffee to warm me up. Once indoors, I found a missed call from a French number on my phone. Curious, I called back, only to hear the familiar voice of an old friend. James had moved to Paris and was now working at one of the French fashion houses. He had called me because the company, La Maison, was undergoing some major changes and he wanted help. They had engaged a few big consultancies to support them with their challenges, but he was now looking for some specialised help in changing behaviours in the organisation.

The company

La Maison had been set up in the 1950s and were known for their haute couture range of products. A few years ago, they were acquired by a large Chinese conglomerate. The acquisition had gone well and the company was profitable. However, one of their senior designers had recently been accused of bullying and a tribunal had ensued in the French courts. La Maison was named in the press and a narrative around high-maintenance fashion designers and their bad behaviour began doing the rounds in the French media. The Chinese owners were unhappy and had required the company to go through mandatory training and policy changes. This created an environment of fear as people were exited from the business and a culture of blame started to emerge.

James said that a new CEO, Max, had been brought in from Singapore to clean up the operation and he understood that the culture of La Maison was at the heart of the problem. James had told Max about us and the work we did in this area, so they decided to call us in to help them think through the culture of La Maison and what could be done to improve it. I mentioned that in order to help them with any work around the culture, we would first need to understand their current culture and identify what some of the features of it were that were both getting in the way and helping them along their strategic journey.

This was an interesting challenge and I immediately got on the phone to Trevor and another colleague, Francis. We came up with a plan to design a cultural assessment for La Maison to get under the skin of their culture. Whilst incidents of bullying and bad behaviour were being spoken about, we were certain that these were only symptoms. Our hypothesis was that there was something else behind these behaviours and it was essential for us to get to the root of the cultural issues before we started helping to design any interventions.

Francis and I went along to a scheduled presentation call with Max, James, and a few other associates, where we laid out our plans and proposals. It was an engaged call and we had a good conversation about how to proceed. That evening, James called me to say that we had won the job and that we should proceed as soon as possible.

The culture assessment

We designed an assessment process that would take into account different voices from across the organisation. We wanted to elicit those components of the culture that were deeply rooted in and which determined the way in which the organisation worked. These often unconscious, entrenched ways are highly influential in determining organisational behaviour. To do this, we decided to conduct a number of what we called 'storytelling' workshops. Each participant would be asked to draw their response to the question: 'What is it like to work here at La Maison?' Others would be then invited to associate with the pictures without trying to interpret what the owner of each picture was trying to draw. This would bring up a rich repository of narrative data and some common themes would begin to emerge.

Combining all this data, we would be able to put together a composite understanding of the culture of the company. Alongside this, we would also conduct one-on-one narrative interviews with the top leadership team to get their views on the culture as well.

We formed a team of four on our way to Paris on the Eurostar. The train was strangely quiet that morning; the press was starting to break stories about the spread of the Covid-19 virus to Europe. A few people were wearing masks and the smell of hand disinfectant hung in the air.

The idea was that Francis would lead the senior team interviews with a co-consultant and I would run the workshops. For me, Paris is always magical and as we drove down the Avenue de Montaigne, the realisation that we were going to work in a fashion house in the heart of Paris began to dawn on me. The normally bustling streets were a lot quieter than usual. The taxi parked outside what looked like a Parisian townhouse. There were no markings or signs on the door except for a security doorbell. We rang the bell, introduced ourselves, and the door smoothly swung open.

Inside was a bare room with what seemed like a black wall, on which were displayed big silver letters that spelled out 'La Maison'. The room was quiet and dimly lit. We waited, not entirely sure of the protocol. And then suddenly a door in the black wall swung open and the noise and bustle of the office flooded the room. James was standing at the doorway and welcomed us in. People were rushing around with papers, fabric, cut-outs, and mannequin body parts. A woman in a corner glass office was screaming into her telephone. Rows of mood boards were displayed along one of the walls and a group of designers were pouring over the details of these. It was pandemonium! We, the consulting team, looked at each other and knew we were all thinking the same thing: 'It's like stepping into an issue of *Vogue*.' This was going to be an exciting job.

Over a period of a week we spoke to over 150 employees in a number of workshops. We also interviewed a number of senior leaders one to one and had a chance to observe the workings of the business. The week was fun, hectic, and high energy. This was juxtaposed with the rising anxiety in France with a number of Covid-19 cases being reported, and rumours of a lockdown doing the rounds. As we boarded the Eurostar back to London that Friday, we commented on how exhausted we were all feeling. We discussed our experiences of the week and I reflected on a curious observation: every time the designers were in the room during the workshops, others would defer to them. The designers were loud, flamboyant, and their voices held weight. Francis commented that he had interviewed the head designer, a lady in her sixties. He said she was frightening, dominating, and dismissive of the process. He remarked on how similar his experience of her was to our experience of her team. We then decided to park our reflections and enjoy a celebratory drink on the train journey home.

Upon returning to London, we quickly scheduled a consulting team workshop to sift through the data and make sense of what was going on. Trevor had flown into London from South Africa and joined this group.

Through our discussions that morning, we started noticing themes emerging from the data. There were a number of good things about La Maison: its brand, the capability of its people, the strong heritage it had, and its leading-edge products. We also found a number of tensions in the data: a pull towards nostalgia versus excitement over the future, a strong tension between the design teams and the production teams, conflict between France and China, and a tension between the leadership and the rest of the organisation.

We wrote all this up and I scheduled a meeting with Max and James the following week to go and present the findings, in preparation for a number of sense-making and design workshops with the client that had been scheduled following this process. That evening, the news of the pandemic hit us with full force.

The big disruption

This would prove to be one of the biggest disruptions in our generation. The Covid-19 pandemic had escalated very quickly in Italy and was beginning to take hold on the rest of the continent. Europe was beginning to close its doors and so began the protracted lockdown that dictated all our lives for the months to come. Trevor managed to get on the late-night flight back to South Africa.

This all meant that I would not be able to travel to Paris to speak to Max and James in person and also that the future of the whole project was in jeopardy. James decided that we should keep the momentum going by having our meeting through a video conference call, and we discussed the findings of the assessment and our plan for the next steps. The day before the scheduled workshop, the UK announced its own complete lockdown. This meant that we had to quickly repurpose our programme of work to ensure we could carry on without disruption. In consultation with James and Max, we decided to take the entire process online and started designing the parameters for online consultation.

Max was uneasy about the way things would work. The lack of face-to-face workshops meant that a process that was supposed to involve four days of intense work would now be protracted. Also, he was starting to worry that the top team were not aligned and fully behind this piece of work. Max was also conflicted over how to involve others in the organisation. What he didn't want to do was to get only the executive team to do the work and thus reinforce the split between the leadership versus the rest of the organisation that we had discovered. He decided to put a working group together that would consist of a couple of participants from his executive team and a few other senior representatives from the rest of the organisation.

I redesigned the process and changed the validation workshops into ten online dialogue sessions with the working group. The purpose of these sessions was to make sense of the assessment of the culture, identify problem areas, and then lay out a plan for intervention. I would do this with a team of consultants. I also set up a coaching and team alignment initiative for Max. Trevor would support him and his executive team in becoming more aligned and in working together as a leadership team. All this would be done remotely, as Trevor was now based in South Africa.

The Covid-19 situation brought with it even more complications than we anticipated. The remoteness from the client and also from each other meant that we were more disconnected than usual. And, in order to connect more, we found ourselves caught up in a manic cycle of work—both with this client and with others. We found ourselves consumed with online meetings, teleconferences, and long workdays. We heard from La Maison that they found themselves in a similar position. The idea that engaging in a manic consumption of tasks would somehow shield us from the anxieties of the pandemic was all around us; a sort of defence mechanism had kicked in.

Ajit and the dialogue sessions

We got the ten dialogue sessions underway and immediately noticed the readiness with which the working group became involved in the process. The group dived right in straightaway. Max was present throughout their journey, yet gave the group a wide berth to allow them to really engage with the material. He said in private that he thought it was important for them to take ownership of the work.

The group re-envisioned a future for La Maison. They worked through some of the non-negotiable behaviours that they wanted to see in the organisation. Finally, they designed a plan to disseminate this information and engage the rest of the organisation in a dialogue.

We were struck by how pleasant the whole experience had been. There had been few robust challenges and the group seemed to have made decisions swiftly. Once we finished the process, we put together a plan for future interventions which we intended to present to the executive team.

I had touched base with Trevor throughout this process to update him on progress with the working group and also to learn how his own work with the executive team was going. I had mentioned that, ultimately, we should aim to bring the whole executive team together to get agreement and alignment around the proposed approach to their organisational culture. We agreed at the time that this was the answer. However, a piece of information confused me: Trevor seemed to be suggesting that the executive team was not fully aware of what was going on in the working group. Given that Max and one of the executive team members were both a part of this group, I was curious as to why they had not reported back to the executive team.

Trevor and the executive alignment process

Ajit had asked me to start working with Max and the rest of the executive team. The task was to build alignment and to get the team to work together cohesively. Max and I had our first teleconference to lay out his expectations and to get to know each other. It was a very collaborative and engaged meeting, with Max sharing a lot of his own thoughts on his executive team. I liked Max and felt really comfortable that we could work together well; the only thing that struck me was that he did not have a strong gut feeling about the underlying culture. But how could he? He was new to the organisation and hearing about a culture is different to experiencing it.

The first executive meeting was fruitful. The team was able to align quite quickly around what they needed to do over the next year to move the organisation forward. They were a new team and were clear that they needed to have their fingers on the pulse of what was happening in the organisation. They spoke a lot about how they would achieve this now as a 'virtual' team and the robustness of their conversation was impressive. I was similarly impressed at how Max was able to give the team space to debate and bump up against each other.

What was strange was that Max presented the culture and values piece to the team as if it were something that *he* had worked on, and I was left wondering why. Jean-Pierre, the CFO, had also been in the working group with Max, but did not speak up. The executive team took up the task of throwing the culture and values piece around with gusto and a fruitful conversation ensued. I decided not to comment on Max and Jean-Pierre's omission, as the team were using the conversation in a manner that was nevertheless unifying and aligning. The team finished the session eager to continue the conversation the following week.

Max called me after the session in such an upbeat mood that I decided not to comment on what he had done with the culture and values piece. I did not want to take away from the energy and enthusiasm that he was filled with. We planned the next session and Max began talking about the idea of an executive team build offsite. I thought that, with lockdown in place, this was overambitious but hypothesised that Max was thinking in this way out of hope.

The next few executive meetings went extremely well: the team commented on how they were enjoying the reflective space, and how it was helping them to work together. They also talked about how the executive meetings were helping to make their one-on-one engagements with each other easier. We spent quite some time planning the executive team building offsite. I was smiling inside as I was unsure whether they were aware that the planning of the team build was actually building the team. I actively looked forward to these sessions.

What was interesting to me was how my conversations with Ajit and Francis about the work became more and more confusing. They spoke with a lot of enthusiasm about the working group and what they were planning in terms of their next steps. I spoke enthusiastically about how the executive team sessions were going and how the planning for the workshop was going. I had the feeling at times that we were talking about different pieces of consulting work in different organisations. Occasionally in our conversations, I found myself feeling defensive and wanting to take the side of the executive team. It felt as though my two colleagues were critical of the work that this team was doing. This needed to be spoken about, as we had a planning meeting coming up with Max and the HR team, and we needed to be aligned.

Ajit and the integration process

I was aware that Trevor was doing work with the executive team and that this was going very well. I called a meeting for the entire consulting team to come together to plan the next steps of the process. When everyone got together, it became apparent that the two parts of this consulting team were split. What I mean is that we were not on the same page in terms of what the objectives of the assignment were.

Trevor passionately made the case for the executive team, whilst I became irritated that the work done in the working group was not being taken into account. We found ourselves in a position where we were struggling to reach a shared understanding of what the purpose of this engagement was. I accused Trevor of going native and he told me that I was not sufficiently connecting parts of the programme. He steadfastly believed that his primary task—what he was there to do— was to create an integrated and cohesive executive team. And this was surprising, as I had on multiple occasions spoken about the different pieces of work and how they related to each other. We were left curious as to what had got into us, the consulting team, and what this represented in the client system.

'Supervision conversation'—or review

In the instance of our work with La Maison, even though we were both involved in events, we used the format of a peer supervision conversation to make sense of what had happened, so that we could then plan the next steps of the programme.

Ajit: Trevor, I was really surprised at our lack of common understanding. I thought I had laid out the vision and purpose multiple times for this programme. Somehow, it seems to have got lost.

Trevor: That is so interesting as I heard that my role was to align and integrate the executive team. Actually, the primary task was to work with the culture and values piece and not to do a purely developmental piece for the executive team.

Ajit: Yes, the developmental piece was a way in, a secondary outcome in order to align them behind the culture and values programme. The piece of data that struck me was that Max and Jean-Pierre did not bring back anything from the working group to the executive team. Unconsciously, it seems as though they have kept the two parts of this process separate.

Trevor: I don't think it was wholly unconscious. Perhaps at a conscious level they wanted to maintain their alliances. It feels as though they would have been cheating on either group if they took information across the boundaries. The relationships on either side of the boundaries are not strong enough. The executive team is new and the working group is new, so there were no foundations of strong relationships on either side. Which means this was a difficult position for Max and Jean-Pierre. Perhaps they had to save face for both the groups they were part of. What I mean is, they couldn't go to the executive team and talk about the messiness of the working group's process, and they couldn't tell the working group that the executive team was not aligned.

Ajit: So, then, what happened to us? Are we saying that in this process we got split because of the systemic dynamics? Did the competition between the two groups end up amongst us as well? My saying to you that you have 'gone native' is an accusatory and almost persecutory thing. I remember saying to you that you had done a fantastic job with Max and his team, as that was the feedback I had received from them. But soon after, it felt to me that I was not being listened to in terms of the primary task of this project.

Trevor: I lost track of the primary task. Instead, my primary focus became building the executive team. And, in effect, you and the working group became 'the other'. So, when you reminded me, and now I recall, multiple times, about the primary task, I was unable to engage as I was focused solely on the executive team. And I think that, in effect, the relationship between us is a microcosm of the executive team and the rest of the organisation. What is playing out here is exactly what our assessment process revealed, which was the big split between the executive team and the rest of La Maison.

Ajit: I agree. It feels as though, somehow, we have become distanced from each other and the consulting team has become split. If we carry on like this, the danger is that we will continue in a disintegrated way, pushing the client system to engage in multiple tasks that will further reinforce the split. What we now need to do is to integrate our way of working, our purpose, and our work in order for this to start affecting the system. My suggestion is that we go to the next meeting together— you, me, and Francis. Let's not engage the system in separate ways, leaving us open to being further split. This way, the client will see us as one and we will be able to do work in different parts of the system with the same primary task in mind.

What next?

We sat down together as a team to define the primary task. We agreed that what we were there to do was to help La Maison build their culture and create an environment that would allow the organisation to flourish. This might have meant multiple activities. However, all these activities must be in service of the primary task. We put this together in an integrated proposal, which included the executive team alignment, a roll-out of the new values, building leadership capability, and so on. However, what was different this time was that we had worked together to determine the course of action aligned throughout to our primary question: 'How can we help La Maison build their culture?'

Given the Covid-19 complexities, we decided to host a video conference. This time, Ajit would not be the only one facing the client when it came to speaking about the next phases of the work. The three of us—Trevor, Ajit, and Francis—planned our strategy before engaging with the client group. We did not want to be split in the meeting and wanted to focus on the primary aim of the consulting work. We agreed that Ajit would play facilitator/orchestrator and Trevor and Francis would offer viewpoints based on their experience of working in the system.

The meeting was between Max, Jean-Pierre, Linda (who was the chair of the working group), and the consultant team. And the purpose of the meeting was to agree the next steps.

Very quickly into the meeting, an interesting incident occurred. A point of contention arose around one of the activities in the next phase. Max seemed to be confused and disagreed with the plan. Linda, on the other hand, had a different view of this and wanted to go with what we were suggesting. Max quickly drew on his relationship with Trevor to get him to agree and support his viewpoint. And Linda pulled on the work that Ajit and Francis had done in the working group to support her argument.

Equipped with the insights gained from our reflective conversation, Trevor realised that a splitting process was happening in the room: a parallel process between the executive team and the working group once again. Rather than agreeing with Max or disagreeing with Linda, Trevor helped them to process the confusion by remaining curious about their opinions. Trevor was aware that by agreeing with either he might end up colluding with them. By taking a neutral stance, he created a space of integration between the two viewpoints. What we demonstrated was that the consulting team would not be split and also that we were focused on the bigger question, which was around building the right culture for La Maison.

This led to a very engaged discussion around how to build a programme of work that brought into account all the parts of the system. From the perspective of the iceberg analogy, we designed an integrated culture programme that would begin by aligning the executive team, enabling the organisation to understand the new desired behaviours and providing leadership with the capability to create the right environment; and finally we would put in place the top-of-iceberg structures that would support the new culture.

La Maison was now on a journey of development. By helping them focus on both the tangible and intangible aspects of the journey, we were able to set in motion a transition process that was holistic and integrated. This meant that they were no longer in danger of being derailed by what they couldn't see.

8. Milan

I t was a hot summer's day when I (Ajit) landed in Milan. It was a long journey from London thanks to the many airport delays, and I had been going over the presentation that I was about to make at CitiCo Technologies. As I drove from the airport, I was filled with anticipation as to how the client would react to what I was about to show them. My team had spent weeks engaging in an exploration of the culture of the firm and I was on my way to share my findings with Marcello, the CEO.

The setting and the players

Marcello had founded a successful software solutions business in Milan in the 1990s. In the early 2000s, an American software development firm (The Group) acquired the business and used it as their gateway into the European market. Marcello had been retained as the CEO as he was seen to be critical to the success of the business. The Italian organisation had been through significant growth and change over the past few years. In 2012, they had bought an artificial intelligence business, brought in new streams of revenue, and increased the size of the business to 400 employees (from 50 in the 1990s). It was one of the success stories of the IT bubble in the 2000s in Italy, having survived what was a very difficult period in the industry.

Marcello was now a successful entrepreneur in his late fifties. He thought on his feet and was very passionate about his business. He was extremely protective of who he brought into his organisation and was a very hands-on leader. We had previously engaged with him right in the middle of a restructuring crisis and had helped him and his business through that tough period. This could be why he had thought about calling us in to work with the business again, as the firm was going through another cycle of change.

His human resources director (HRD), Anna, had been with him since the beginning. She was also in her late fifties and, by her own admission, was like the quintessential Italian *nonna* of the business. Marcello and Anna got along very well, and he leaned on her for support and advice on important decisions.

My consulting team and I agreed with Marcello to conduct an initial exploratory exercise to get an understanding of the current business and some of the challenges they faced. We planned to speak to all the senior leaders in the business and then to formulate a plan. We agreed to meet again in a month to discuss our findings. We felt that by engaging in a shared task of analysis, interpretation, and insight, we could build a collaborative diagnostic of what was going on.

We spoke to each of the leaders in the business. Everyone was forthcoming and participated in the interviews. We also spent some time observing behaviour on the shop floor and spoke with small groups of employees across the business. From this, we formulated a picture of what we thought was going on.

The presentation

Marcello and Anna met me and my team in reception with a hug and warm welcome. Marcello was in an excitable mood; he was talking about football and his recent golfing adventures in Portugal. We were taken straight up to the executive boardroom—a flash, swanky space kitted out with all the latest technology. It had panoramic glass windows that overlooked the city. Once we had settled in, Marcello said, 'Right, so tell me what you found.'

I had practised the presentation in my head during the flight and I knew that my team was well prepared too. We highlighted a number of key themes to Marcello. However, he got stuck on the very first point. We said that there seemed to be a lack of clarity about the overall business strategy across the organisation. We had found that individuals felt lost in the organisation as they did not fully understand the overall goals of the business and where it was going.

Marcello was visibly enraged. He thumped his fist on the table and said that he totally disagreed with us. At first, we were surprised by his reaction. He said that he had taken the entire business away on multiple strategy awaydays and therefore everyone should know the strategy by now. He was quick to dismiss our finding and immediately wanted us to tell him who in the organisation was saying this. We pointed out that it would be unfair to name people but that this was a consistent theme that had emerged from all our data collection. This angered him even further. He said he was tired of hearing about how things were not running smoothly in his business when he had been hard to ensure that everyone understood his vision for the future.

At this point, I reflected privately that my team and I had worked with him for many years and this behaviour was extremely uncharacteristic of him. So I intervened and said, 'We can see you are very upset by this. Can you help us understand what you are angry about?' This seemed to diffuse the situation and he started opening up about his frustrations.

He said that he had expended a lot of time and effort over the past year on educating everyone in the business about his vision. He had asked his senior leadership team (SLT) to work with their teams to build individual strategies aligned with his overall vision for the whole business. He said that after all he had done, to hear our feedback made him very angry. We explored this even further with him and asked him whether he was angry with what he had heard, or angry at his SLT for not delivering on his instructions. He thought about this for a while and then reflected that he did not think they were a true team. He felt they were a group of people who worked together. Anna, who was sitting beside him, looked at him and they gave each other a knowing look, rolled their eyes, and shrugged their shoulders.

They then proceeded to tell us that each of the businesses had built their individual strategies as independent silos and had not really aligned them with the overall picture, something we had picked up on in our conversations with the SLT. We probed further and he went on to say that he did not feel like they were a strong next generation. He felt that those below the SLT were the new talent in the business and were much more capable. We asked him who was named to succeed him when he retired, and he said that they had a successor on paper, but he was not convinced it was the right choice. He did not think anyone in his leadership team could lead the business in his absence.

We asked him if he had spoken about this with his team and he deflected the conversation back to how he felt we had misdiagnosed the problem. He insisted that we change our view around the awareness of strategy in the organisation and accordingly change our intervention plan. He then left the meeting in a hurry, leaving Anna to finish up as he said she had the details of a piece of work that he wanted us to prioritise.

The urgent intervention

Anna was very extremely welcoming from the start. She had spent time with us, introducing us to the organisation and ensuring that we were appropriately inducted into the firm. Anna was very strict about ensuring the culture was intact and was steadfastly loyal to the organisation's brand and values. She described herself as the person who others came to if they wanted a shoulder to cry on or reassurance, or if someone needed to be 'told off' and 'put straight'.

Anna said now that she wanted us to roll out training for the whole business around managing performance. We questioned the purpose of this, and she said that it was her view that the SLT did not drive good feedback behaviours in their teams and were not managing performance appropriately. She felt that we would be able to solve the problem as we knew the characters well and that a consistent 'sheep-dip' training for everyone would help establish a consistent language and methodology across the organisation. Her understanding was that people were not having feedback conversations across the business. As a result, she felt that a lot of bad behaviour and poor performance was going unchecked. We alerted her that a training programme was not going to change this and that it required a deeper cultural interrogation. We asked whether we could work with her to understand first why this was happening, before jumping to the training solution. She was adamant that we must begin with the training and then, out of that, other things could follow. It was clear that she was not prepared to negotiate with us over this.

We agreed with Anna to raise the proposal at the next SLT meeting. Along with providing some tools and language, we would get them to start role-modelling this behaviour. We suggested that as a part of our consulting work, we could work with each of the teams to embed the behaviours that we would be working on during the workshops. This would link in nicely with the work on culture that we had been brought in to do and we could tie all the interventions together. Anna agreed and we left with a plan in place.

The final showdown

We spent a lot of time working out an appropriate immersive design for this intervention. We took into account some of the findings from our exploratory phase and incorporated these into the way the workshops would run. That way, we felt we would start the intervention process and use the workshops as a vehicle to effect the change required.

We flew back to Milan a few weeks later having prepared for a week of back-to-back delivery. Before we started the workshops, we had a meeting with the SLT and agreed that they would sponsor them. In other words, at each workshop, an SLT member would be present to participate and model the behaviour they expected from others. We also agreed that they would encourage their teams to attend. On my recommendation, Marcello sent out an all-staff email saying that, based on feedback received, he was commissioning this exercise as a part of a larger initiative to encourage a more open, dialogue-based and performance-focused environment in the firm.

We spent the week running workshop after workshop. They were exhausting and hard work but the participants who attended spoke highly about the facilitation and commended us on making the content relevant to them. At the end of the sessions, the feedback about the content and delivery was very good. A curious thing happened, however; the members of the SLT did not attend the sessions as agreed. Nor did they encourage their people to attend. And, at times, they did not allow their staff time off from their day jobs to attend. I raised this with both

Marcello and Anna at our final closeout meeting before we left Milan. They did not seem concerned about this and were happy with the comments they read in the feedback forms.

Guillotined

The annual performance review cycle came around a few months later. I had an urgent call from Anna. She said that many staff were complaining that they had not had good feedback conversations with their managers. The performance process was seen to be a tick-box exercise. There were questions raised about the value of the conversations and old behaviours had not changed. Anna blamed us for lack of delivery, saying that the training had not worked.

I pointed out to Anna that she had to raise this at the leadership level as they had taken accountability to sponsor this process. We had said that they must model the behaviours they wanted to see. Therefore, it would be useful to challenge the SLT and ask them why they did not fully stand by the process.

After all, the intervention was about feedback and she must provide feedback to the team around their behaviour. We also alerted her to our initial warning that training would not solve the issue and that there were other underlying factors and dynamics at play. She did not want to listen to our intervention and instead threatened to withhold payment for the work. I tried to reach out to Marcello soon after, but he was unavailable to talk to me. I decided to let the dust settle before reaching out again.

Consultant's reflections

As we reflected on our engagements with this client, we started to think about what was deep-rooted in the system that caused them to behave in this way. We were struck by their inability to confront issues. This was at all levels of the organisation and was symptomatic of how they operated with each other. In both situations, we—the consulting team— seemed to play a significant role in highlighting this, and, in doing so, we had probably made them face their anxieties. However, instead of managing their anxiety, our behaviour seemed to have exacerbated it by calling it out. By doing this, we were able to get more data on the underlying dynamics, from which we started forming the following two hypotheses.

Our first hypothesis was that Marcello had created an SLT that was impotent and incapable of 'killing him off'. He had created a huge dependency on him. Could it be that Marcello unconsciously kept the SLT in a weak position so they would not overthrow him? The SLT, in turn, unconsciously played out this dynamic by not fully carrying out his instructions on how to build the business as a whole. Instead, they were concerned only with their individual areas of responsibility. They seemed to sabotage the overall organ-isational purpose, concerning themselves instead with their own profit and loss accounts. This was evident in how they dealt with the all-business learning intervention put in place by Anna, which was seen as a distraction by them.

We, the consulting team, were aware of the potential set-up and steadfastly stuck to our boundaries, holding up a mirror to Marcello. However, it was possible that in running the workshops we found ourselves in the middle of a conflict in the leadership team. By sabotaging the intervention and not showing up, the SLT were in effect attacking Marcello himself.

We wondered whether there was some sort of struggle for succession going on. Change creates anxiety. We knew that there was impending change on the horizon and this anxiety could be a source of resistance to it. Perhaps Marcello himself was unconsciously resisting retirement and blaming his SLT and a lack of an obvious successor to give himself licence to stay on? The story reminded us of the experience with Rajat in Mumbai; there was a similar theme of transition in the narrative. Something was being avoided and in trying to uncover this we were being attacked. It was a painful experience that we couldn't fully make sense of in the moment.

Supervision conversation

Trevor: Marcello, like many successful entrepreneurs or founders, appears to have driven the business from the front. The way in which you describe the success of the business points to Marcello's personal abilities. When hearing you describe the story, I am left wondering about Marcello's view of his own abilities and his awareness of them. It is understandable, and commonplace, that founder leaders surround themselves with teams who are task-focused and execute their strategy. This unfortunately leaves a layer of leadership missing in these organisations.

Ajit: I completely agree with you. The SLT were running their departments as little fiefdoms and, as such, were dependent on Marcello to hold the 'whole' organisation in mind. The SLT was not a team; they were a group of individuals who worked together. Marcello, whilst a very benevolent leader, was also caught up in his own narrative about how he had created this business from nothing and was very proud of his achievement. So, it makes sense that he was protective of the company.

Trevor: Well, have you come across a business that has only ever been built by one person? It feels as though within his narrative it is all about him and not all those who helped him to build the business. Reflecting the experience of the SLT back to Marcello, and providing a soft systems diagnosis, I get the sense that he believes that you have placed the blame on him and not on his team. The extent of his rage points clearly to this. Though your interpretation is in all likelihood true, you have injured him. When you move back to mirroring his feelings, you repair the relationship and he settles—again diagnostically important for looking at Marcello's personality.

Ajit: Marcello responded to me like he had just been told off. I experienced his rage as a rejection of my analysis. I believe I did touch a nerve by pointing this out and I also believe that he knew this, but my vocalising it possibly made it too difficult for him to hear in the moment. His rage was a defence against what was possibly a premature intervention.

Trevor: Yes, Marcello appears to still require collusion rather than accurate interpretation. I'm really curious what his fantasies were about how your consulting would unfold, and how in his mind he felt you disappointed him. This provides a real dilemma for you as a consulting team. How do you remain empathically attuned and curious and simultaneously not collude? Also, a question to consider here is what function does the pairing between Anna and Marcello perform in the organisation?

Ajit: What do you think about Anna and her role in the system?

Trevor: I am wondering if Anna and Marcello make up the traditional parental dyad. I am wondering if she came to Marcello's rescue by ordering you to undertake an impossible and slightly humiliating task of running 'training' on performance management. Someone I really respect once said to me that you can train animals, not people; our consultancy does not do 'training' and therefore you were, in my mind, being undermined.

Ajit: I am now wondering if she set me up to fail. What I mean by this is that she knew I would get behind the problem and engage with it in a process consulting way. Instead, she kept me 'busy' by giving me the training work.

Trevor: Much more than busy—it feels like she punished you for wounding Marcello. From how you describe Anna and the subsequent large number of no-shows for the workshops, it appears that her own requirements were for a maintenance of the status quo.

Ajit: Yes, however, there was also something about how the SLT was sabotaging the planned intervention. She had decided that the organisation needed this training and pushed for the SLT to endorse it. However, they actively undermined it and didn't allow their people to attend.

Trevor: From personal experience, I am aware that the Italian nonna is sweet and benevolent until you cross her or her family. I wonder whether by giving her the feedback that the intervention had not worked because the SLT had not appropriately sponsored it, you attacked her family. In both instances, with Marcello and with Anna, you found yourself in a similar situation where you have held up the mirror and got attacked by the client. Whether the intervention was premature or not is difficult to say. The question is how to speak about the dynamic without activating defence mechanisms. As you well know, once a defence is activated you are not going to break it, even by naming it. My question to you is: how can you help Marcello deal with his impending departure? And, simultaneously, what would this mean for Anna?

Ajit: Perhaps I can utilise the trusted advisor relationship with Marcello and Anna to help them visualise a future for the organisation without them in it. This would put the current SLT in the driving seat and not reinforce the anxieties that Marcello and Anna currently hold, which is what I think both interventions have currently done.

Trevor: Absolutely! By lowering their defences through an empathically attuned consultation, this may have been a powerful catalyst for organisational change. You may also unlock something in the SLT by breaking Marcello and Anna's reinforcing beliefs that the SLT is not 'good enough'.

What next?

Armed with these insights, I decided to fly over to Milan to have lunch with Marcello and Anna. I sent them an email saying that I was coming over and that I had had some thoughts about the next steps in this process. I suggested that I take them out to lunch and that we spend some time debriefing the work up so far. I said in my email that I had some suggestions for the next steps, and it was up to them if they would like to consider them.

I was surprised by the speed of their response, as they both immediately agreed. Marcello insisted that we meet at a restaurant of his choice and that we would be his guests. Anna then wrote back warmly, saying that a car had been arranged to collect us from the airport and that the two of them would meet me and my colleague at the restaurant. She added that they were grateful that we were taking the time and making the effort to fly over to see them.

I was filled with anxiety on the flight and my colleague and I spoke of how we would play it. Reflecting on our experience, we agreed that we would at first just listen, ask them questions and only offer them anything when we felt they were ready to listen.

Anna and Marcello were already seated at the table when we arrived. They were welcoming as usual. After some initial pleasantries, they looked to us to start the meeting. I asked them how they were doing and what was happening for them. Marcello launched into a long reflection on the business and his leadership team. He said how disappointed he was in the team that they had not supported the intervention that we had worked on. He seemed despondent. Anna supported his reflections and went on to say how she felt she was constantly firefighting. They seemed exhausted, but said they couldn't move on as they couldn't leave the business in the state it was.

Instead of offering any solutions, we spent most of the lunch helping them make sense of this anxiety. They were starting to see how they were both grieving Marcello's impending departure. We began talking about what they and the business stood to gain or lose from the impending change. This changed the texture of the conversation. They were able to locate themselves in the future and start to recognise what the transition would look like. We helped them reflect on what they felt the organisation must be going through in the knowledge that its founder was to soon retire.

This insight into some of the anxieties in the system was useful for them. Together, we concluded that in order to move forward we needed to help the organisation come to terms with the anxiety of Marcello's departure. We needed to help him appoint a successor who would be able to address this anxiety. And we needed to work with the SLT to resolve some of their internal dynamics; those with each other and with Marcello. This would become the focus of the consulting work.

At the time of writing this piece, Marcello has announced his departure date. He has also appointed a successor and an eighteen-month transition period is underway. We are working with the leadership team to strengthen their relationships with each other. We are also working with the successor to help him establish his authority and leadership. And, finally, we are working with Marcello to help him disentangle himself from being a CEO and take on more of a mentoring role for the organisation in the transition.

Reflections on our journey

The writing of this book has been a learning process in itself. We have had supervision ('extravision') conversations, written chapters, got caught up with client engagements and our own personal lives, and then come back to the chapters with a different lens. This has led to deeper and sometimes difficult and challenging conversations that have in turn led to numerous chapter revisions. The process and nature of our engagements have created more psychological safety and therefore allowed us to go deeper into the work. We have experienced disruptions in our relationship through writing this book and have, through that relationship, repaired those disruptions. For this is the nature of good relationships. Much like when a broken bone repairs, it is way stronger at the point of the original break, so strong and textured relationships require constant disruptions and repairs.

It has become much clearer for us both through this process how limited a singular individual viewpoint is in any situation. Each of us perceives each situation we enter through our own 'lens', which develops through our lifelong experiences. This 'lens' can only ever capture a small part of the entire experience—our own part, which is mediated and made sense of through our own experiences. Our perspectives are therefore never 'objective' whole views. In other words, as the writer Anaïs Nin said, 'We don't see things as they are, we see them as we are.' The 'other' person we are in relationship with—be they a client, co-consultant, a peer, a subordinate, or a boss—sees the same situation through their own lens. It is through the combination and interrogation of these views (if we are open to that process), and if we can give up the position of wishing to appear all-knowing, that a more rounded, fuller panorama of what might actually be happening emerges. This is known as the intersubjective space. This book is, in itself, the 'intersubjective space' of our consulting experiences. It is also an invitation to you, the reader, to examine your own underlying assumptions of what might be happening in your own organisation or consulting interventions.

To undertake such a journey of self exploration in a leadership role is by no means easy. We have grown up in a society that has created the ideal of the all-knowing, all-powerful leader. We only have to look around us to see the 'strong men' leaders of the world who claim to have the answers to the world's problems. We also only have to look at where we currently find ourselves to understand that this type of leadership archetype is merely a myth and has not helped us out of our dilemmas. The 'strong man' leadership archetype struggles to navigate the complex, interconnected world we live in. To work within the 'intersubjective space' requires engaging with our not-knowing as human beings and more specifically as leaders, and trusting in what emerges through relating with others.

In choosing which stories to include in this book, we selected those that posed challenging dilemmas both for us and for our client systems. Often the presenting problem was not the issue we ended up working with, which in turn emphasises the need to be curious and to let go of our own biases when we engage in a consulting relationship.

There are many models of consulting: the expert consultant, for instance, engages in the relationship through the particular expertise they bring to it, say, for example, in a certain area such as financial accounting or management consulting. However, it is our view that those relationships create a dependency on the expert and that this does not always equip the organisation with what it needs to survive and thrive in the consultant's absence.

What we are bringing to the relationship is our expertise in organisations and organisational dynamics. We take up our roles in a particular way; we do not impose our expertise but equip the client to engage with the problem so that they are capable of solving it for themselves. Often, we will provide examples from our experience in order for the client to see how these sorts of problems have been solved previously; however, they are then able to exert their authority in deciding the course of action for their organisation. This is a more challenging and frustrating way of working for clients, as providing an easy answer shortcuts and bypasses the difficult process of grappling with a problem.

And it is this idea of *process* that is paramount, not as a thing but as a way of engaging with a problem and with each other. Process is dialogue—but dialogue with purpose, not dialogue for dialogue's sake. Like a spiral, with every turn there is greater depth of understanding. What is important is that the right people engage in the process.

A principle that we hold very close to our practice is that of curiosity. Often, we feel that we can see the answer in front of our eyes, but by bypassing the notion of process we are disenfranchising the client from learning and growing. And, also, we may not have a full grasp of the problem. The British psychoanalyst Wilfred Bion famously talked about engaging with groups of people 'without memory or desire' (Bion 1961[1]). Whilst he was referring to therapeutic groups, there is application of this in organisational consulting. It is difficult for a consultant to enter a system as a completely blank slate, as we are filled with our own experiences, our own biases—both conscious and unconscious—and the expectations of the client. What we can do, though, is to be aware and acknowledge everything we bring into a consulting relationship, and then use those parts that are most helpful to the client. This requires a level of situational awareness, self-awareness, and humility.

By situational awareness, we are referring to using all of our senses in order to help us become aware of everything that is occurring around us. Much as animal trackers in traditional societies have done for centuries, we use our senses to pay attention to the wider ecosystem we

---

[1] Bion, W. R. (1961). *Experiences in Groups*. London: Tavistock.

are operating within in order to better understand what is happening in an interconnected or 'bigger picture' manner. We need not only to focus on what is happening externally but also on what is happening to us internally. We have found that we have been helped to develop self-awareness by engaging in the supervision process both as peers and as professionals. Supervision has revealed the blind spots in our consulting work and relationships.

And whilst this idea is particularly helpful for consultants, it has resonance with leadership as well. Leaders who are able to listen, stay curious, and create a space where their teams can engage and relate, are more effective. There will be times when leaders need to be decisive and take action; however, if sufficient process has occurred before, this becomes easier and more impactful. And, often, leaders find themselves alone and in situations where there is no precedence. Using other leaders or a coach to work through the circumstances they are facing, to understand their own subjectivity and contributions to a situation, vastly improves leadership ability and capability.

We all have a tendency to go looking for things that we believe we don't have—just like Dorothy and her friends go looking for the Wizard of Oz, when all along they had what they were searching for. We believe our role as consultants is to help our clients with this realisation: that they already possess the resources necessary to engage with the organisational problems they face, as they often don't appreciate this, or they don't know how to set about looking for them.

Our hope in writing this book, and our experience of writing it, is that you, the reader, can find some resonance with the processes of discovery through relationships and conversations that are described in the different consulting stories. We hope that reading these stories has offered you a different perspective and perhaps a small element of the pleasure that they afforded us.

At the time of writing this conclusion, it is now eight weeks since of the beginning of lockdown due to Covid-19 and so much of what we took for granted has disappeared. All of our worlds have changed; the two of us are on different sides of the planet and yet we talk more often than we ever did. Our world of consulting has fundamentally changed; the way we deliver our work has changed but not what we work with. Even though we are based in our homes in different hemispheres, we are working together on client engagements daily and have, like so many others, become 'experts' in virtual working.

What has not changed is what we work with and how we work together. At the base of all our work are ourselves, our fellow human beings, and the relationships between us. The way we relate and collaborate allows us to get things done or gets in the way of things getting done. It is the complexity of the dynamics of these relationships that inhabit the 'below the surface' of the metaphoric iceberg. The world around us might be changing continually but what remains consistent is what humans require from each other in order to get things done. The capacity of humans to band together and collaborate has shown itself through the Covid-19 pandemic. How many of us would have believed that we would have been so compliant to being essentially locked up inside our homes for almost three months in some cases? We have also seen people band together in resistance to change in great numbers. Engaging people's hearts has been shown to be as important, if not more important, as engaging their brains. When the sentiment of the group has turned, the direction of the group simultaneously shifts.

We have witnessed varying degrees of success in terms of leadership through the pandemic, and though there is no doubt some confirmation bias from our side, our underlying assumption—that success in a leadership role is fundamentally about the ability to understand oneself and others, as well being able to build and maintain effective relationships—has proven itself over and over again. We have witnessed leaders who are used to utilising command and control techniques struggle when it comes to leading us through the current crisis. Managing through efficiencies and controls has shown itself to be of less use than managing through relationships in a world of 'lockdown' work from home.

Leaders who have been able to identify their own vulnerabilities and the vulnerabilities of those who work for them, and who have acknowledged these, have created and contained psychologically safe 'virtual' spaces for their teams, which have allowed for the achievement of amazing results. The pandemic has simultaneously shown how tiring the role of relationship-based—or what we often refer to as 'secure base'—leadership can be. Being a secure base for so many people continually is exhausting and has highlighted the need for those in leadership roles to have their own secure bases in order not to burn out. We have seen many leaders who are usually self-reliant reaching out for support and asking for spaces of reflection in order to make sense of what is happening around them. These leaders have noted that in a crisis such as the Covid-19 pandemic, no one has 'knowledge' of what will happen, and this ability to work with uncertainty and 'not-knowing' is leadership gold.

However difficult the experience of the last few months has been, the situation has not at its core been fundamentally different to what leadership is expected to deal with on a continual basis—and that is managing change. Change is an inevitable aspect of life, it occurs consistently and is something that we continually need to work with. Charles Darwin's ideas are often misinterpreted: many think he talked about survival of the fittest, whereas he spoke rather about survival of the most adaptable. Whilst we may have the desire to be in control of what happens in the world around us and within our businesses, we know that this is not possible. What will ensure that we succeed as organisations, as leaders within organisations, and as consultants to organisations, is that we are able to adapt to ongoing changes and disruptions. This means constantly paying attention to what is happening around us and within us; paying attention to not only what happens above the surface but even more so to what is happening beneath the surface of our organisations and ourselves.

Further reading

This list is not exhaustive but rather a starting point for anyone who would like to read more on the subjects that we have spoken about in our stories. We have suggested a few books in each category to help you on your journey of discovery. Some are classics and timeless and others we believe are turning points in the development of the field.

The unconscious and systems psychodynamics

Cardona, F. (2020). *Work Matters: Consulting to Leaders and Organisations in the Tavistock Tradition*. London: Routledge.

Hirschhorn, L. (1990). *The Workplace Within: Psychodynamics of Organizational Life*. Cambridge, MA: MIT Press.

Obholzer, A. & Roberts, V. Z. (Eds.). (2019). *The Unconscious at Work* (2nd ed.). London: Routledge.

Organisation development

French, W. & Bell, C. (1999). *Organization Development: Behavioural Science Interventions for Organization Improvement* (6th ed.). Upper Saddle River, NJ: Prentice-Hall.

Gallos, J. V. (Ed.) (2006). *Organization Development. A Jossey-Bass Reader*. San Francisco, CA: Jossey-Bass.

Organisational culture

Schein, E. H. (2010). *Organizational Culture and Leadership*. San Francisco, CA: Jossey-Bass.

Organisational and leadership coaching

Brunning, H. (Ed.) (2006). *Executive Coaching: Systems-Psychodynamic Perspective*. London: Karnac.

Hawkins, P. (2017). *Leadership Team Coaching: Developing Collective Transformational Leadership*. London: KoganPage.

Kahn, M. S. (2014). *Coaching on the Axis: An Integrative and Systemic Approach to Business Coaching*. London: Karnac.

Leadership

Ghoshal, S. & Bartlett, C. A. (1997). *The Individualized Corporation: A Fundamentally New Approach to Management*. New York, NY: Harper Business.

Kets de Vries, M. (2006). *The Leadership Mystique: Leading Behavior in the Human Enterprise* (2nd ed.) London: Financial Times/Prentice Hall.

Kohlrieser, G., Goldsworthy, S., & Coombe, D. (2012). *Care to Dare: Unleashing Astonishing Potential Through Secure Base Leadership*. San Francisco, CA: Jossey-Bass.

Western, S. (2019). *Leadership: A Critical Text*. Newbury Park, CA: SAGE.

Process consulting

de Haan, E. (2004). *The Consulting Process as Drama: Learning from King Lear*. London: Karnac.

Isaacs, W. (1999). *Dialogue and the Art of Thinking Together*. New York, NY: Doubleday.

Schein, E. (1999). *Process Consultation Revisited: Building the Helping Relationship*. Reading, MA: Addison-Wesley.

Change

Kegan, R. & Lahey, L. L. (2009). *Immunity to Change: How to Overcome It and Unlock the Potential in Yourself and Your Organization*. Boston, MA: Harvard Business.

Kotter, J. P. (1996). *Leading Change*. Boston, MA: Harvard Business.